A Matter Of Destiny

No part of this publication may be reproduced, stored in a retrieval system, or transmitted, in any form or by any means, electronic, mechanical, photocopying, recording, or otherwise without the prior written permission of the author.

Copyright © 2006 Joanne B. Parrotta
All rights reserved.
ISBN:1-4196-5175-7

Library of Congress Control Number: 2006908827

To order additional copies, please contact us.
BookSurge, LLC
www.booksurge.com
1-866-308-6235
orders@booksurge.com

JOANNE B. PARROTTA

A MATTER OF DESTINY
How to Find and Marry Your Soulmate: A Beginner's Spiritual Guide

2006

A Matter Of Destiny

TABLE OF CONTENTS

Introduction   xix

Chapter 1: True Love Never Dies   1
Your Journey Begins — You Have Been Here Before — Free Will Is Our Birthright — What Is Karma and How Does It Affect Us? — Three Types of Soulmates

Chapter 2: Avoiding Relationships That Bring You Down   19
Obsessive Love: The Wrong Kind of Love — When Your Partner Won't Commit — Just Love Is Not Enough — Loving Others without Losing Ourselves — Change Is Difficult — Confidence Is Beautiful

Chapter 3: Preparing to Meet Your Loving Soulmate   37
Doing the Inner Work — Spiritual Health — Look Good to Feel Good — Eat Well to Live Well — Cleanliness Is Next to Godliness

Chapter 4: Manifesting Your Soulmate   49
Making the Dream a Reality — How Your Angels Can Help You Find Your Soulmate — Your Destiny and Your Connection with Your Soulmate

Chapter 5: Meeting Your Wonderful Soulmate 63
How to Recognize Your Loving Soulmate — When and Where Can We Find Our Soulmates?

Chapter 6: Dating in Order to Find Your Soulmate 73
Dating with Confidence — Internet Dating –– Only Fools Rush In –– What to Look For — Characteristics to Avoid — Dating Do's and Don'ts — Dating Safety Tips for Women –– Sexual Responsibility

Chapter 7: So You've Met Your Soulmate 91
What Do Men Really Want? — What Do Women Really Want? — To Have and to Hold –– Before You Say "I Do" — For Better or Worse — Don't Be Afraid to Apologize — Preparing for the Wedding — Some Ways to Say "I Love You" — Unconditional Love: The Key to a Successful Union

Films with Soulmate Themes 107

Bibliography and Recommended Reading 109

ACKNOWLEDGEMENTS

As always, I must begin by thanking God and the Universe for all of my blessings.

Many thanks, to all the wonderful people who have kindly contributed their knowledge, encouragement, and stories. I sincerely appreciate your taking the time to share your thoughts and stories with me.

Much gratitude to my editor, Susan Fitzgerald, for taking my many pages of ramblings and transforming them into English; thank you.

Finally to you the reader, I give thanks that you are allowing me to become a part of your life. I sincerely hope you enjoy this book and use it to make a difference in your life.

IN PRAISE OF
A MATTER OF DESTINY

The author deals with this subject in a sensitive, friendly and easy-to-understand manner. Her passion for helping others to live their best lives is obvious in her writing."

— Susan Fitzgerald, Ph. D.
Editor

"A simple and straightforward guide to finding your mate. A must-read for all young lovers!"

— Susan Harris, B.Ed.
Teacher – Channel – Writer – Speaker

"This is a great book for someone just beginning their spiritual journey. Easy to read and understand and covers a great range of topics. Very highly recommended."

— John Punto

"This book has made a huge difference in my life. Just when I was about to settle for second best, I came across *A Matter of Destiny*. And approximately eight months after ending my relationship with the man I came close to marrying, I met my loving soulmate. This book has changed my life."

— Joan A.

"Dear Joanne, Thanks for writing this book. I have learned

so much about myself. I now have the confidence I need to step up my search for my true love. Thank you for giving me hope once again."

— Laura Lee

DEDICATION

I Lovingly Dedicate This Book To My Wonderful Children Who Helped Inspire A Matter Of Destiny. I Am So Very Proud Of All Of You. You Are My Reason For Being And Persevering And I Am Truly Blessed To Have You In My Life. I Would Also Like To Dedicate This Book To My Nieces And Nephews (Too Many To Mention). This Book Is My Gift To You.

Love You All!

INTRODUCTION

It exists in the depths of our souls. It appears in our dreams. Although some may not care to admit it, the hope of finding our one true love lies within us all. The term *soulmate* is often trivialized, but when used in its proper context, it describes the profound love of which our dreams are made and which our souls crave to discover. Most of us are searching for such a relationship—one that goes deeper than physical attraction and beyond our highest expectations, creating the union of two minds and two souls.

We intuitively know when our relationships—past or even present—are lacking an important element. We often wonder if there can be more to a relationship than what we repeatedly experience. Imagine finally meeting your meant-to-be love. Envision finding that one person who is truly ever present and whose dedication and love are unconditional. By opening this book, you have taken a step toward finding this special someone.

These relationships are highly misunderstood, and controversy and confusion surround them. Some claim that soulmates come into our lives only to cause turmoil and misery, while others believe that our soulmates await us in the spirit world. Some believe that we have but one true soulmate who will complete us, while others believe that we have many soulmates with whom we can connect spiritually. Still others do not believe in soulmates at all. You must not let your curiosity be curbed by sceptics who claim that soulmate relationships do not exist. Do not allow others to crush your belief in soulmates and don't let them shatter your dream of meeting your true love.

In this book I clarify some of the uncertainty surrounding the concept of soulmates. Although I don't consider myself an expert and don't claim to have all the answers (nor, I believe, does anyone), I do know that your ultimate partner is not a fantasy—he or she is real. How do I know this? I guess you can say my belief in soulmates comes from within—a gut feeling—as well as from personal experiences, observations, and years of extensive research and study, as well as from many seminars and countless conversations with spiritual experts.

I have spent years working in the beauty industry and it is well known that clients share the intimate details of their private lives with their beauticians. Through many such conversations, I have been exposed to unhealthy and unhappy relationships and have met numerous people who strove to find their one true-life partner.

Although many people are single by choice, just as many would love to meet that special someone, but for one reason or another have not been successful in doing so. My motivation for writing this book is to help these people find their loving soulmates and settle into a committed relationship or marriage. I hope to give them the tools they need to stop choosing incompatible partners, and instead, to attract, recognize, and keep their destined love in their lives.

We all want to avoid falling in love with—and especially marrying—the wrong person. The divorce rate is now more than a staggering 50 percent (and that's not to mention all those couples who stay together not because they are in love, but for the sake of their children, money, status, etc). We need to be more cautious; the choice of a lifelong mate will determine whether or not our lives will be happy or miserable. A large part (experts believe about 90 percent) of our happiness relies on this decision alone.

Even though *A Matter of Destiny* is a spiritual guide to attracting and keeping your soulmate, you do not have to believe in spiritualism to benefit from this book. Everyone, regardless of religious or spiritual convictions—or lack thereof—can still find their soulmates. The central truth that links all religious and spiritual beliefs is love. After all, all religions are supposed to lead their believers to eternal love, are they not?

This book is so much more than a guide for finding your spiritual partner. I also discuss dating in order to find your soulmate, obsessive love (the wrong kind of love), and many more matters related to love relationships.

I have purposely written this book in an easy-to-read and understandable format, unlike many books on this topic which require an interpreter to make sense of them. *A Matter of Destiny* is written for single men and women who are just beginning to realize that there must be something more to love relationships than what they have been experiencing.

You may be wondering why I feel qualified to offer relationship advice. After all, I am not a licensed counsellor or therapist (although I have had some training and consider myself a counsellor at heart). I am not even a professional writer. Writing books is not something I set out to do; I didn't even start writing until I was in my early forties.

In fact, my formal education is limited; school was never my thing. But over the years I have been working hard to catch up. I have been an avid reader for the past twenty years, which has helped me tremendously with my writing. I am a normal person who developed a strong passion for this subject about ten years ago and has been studying and writing about it ever since.

I write motivational books, articles, and reports in plain English. They are easy to understand and concise (which means I get right to the point), and therefore quick, easy, and enjoyable to read. I don't use unnecessary fillers to bulk up the book. I know how busy you are.

The topics I write about are inspired by my children (now young adults); I write about subjects such as the importance of good health, natural nutrition, living a balanced life, spirituality, and of course, relationships, in order to help them learn and to make their lives a little easier, happier, and more fulfilling. I guess you can say my books are a legacy that I will leave my family when I leave this earth. I can't think of a better way to continue to share my wisdom, guidance, and advice with my loved ones. And although my children inspire the topics, I write for anyone who would like to benefit from my knowledge and research.

Okay, now that we've gotten that out of the way, let's get back to the subject at hand. How you can find your meant-to-be love and settle into a committed relationship or marriage? If you are ready to take the next step, or even if you are considering whether or not you are ready to find your mate, I invite you to embark on the journey to a wonderful lifetime of love that can begin here and now.

May love's sweetest miracle touch each and every one of you!

With love and blessings,
Joanne B. Parrotta

SONG OF SOLOMON

3:2–4

I will rise now, and go about the city in the streets, and in the broad ways I will seek him whom my soul loveth: I sought him, but I found him not.
The watchmen that go about the city found me: to whom I said, Saw ye him whom my soul loveth?
It was but a little that I passed from them, but I found him whom my soul loveth: I held him, and would not let him go.

CHAPTER 1
TRUE LOVE NEVER DIES

Within these pages, you will find a valuable stepping-stone leading you closer to the love that awaits you. As I mentioned in the introduction, there are many opinions about what soulmates are or if they even exist. In this chapter, I will address the confusion surrounding the subject, providing you with the confidence and knowledge that will guide your path to your spiritual partner.

I believe that people seek their loving soulmates when their spiritual sides awaken. They start to yearn for something more then a normal relationship. If you are one of these people, it is to you especially that I speak in this book.

Your soulmate is searching and longing for you, just as much as you are seeking and yearning for him or her. You are reading these words because, whether you know it or not, something spectacular is about to happen to you. This book has been brought to your attention because you are meant to reunite with your beloved. There are no coincidences in life. Every moment and every event, no matter how miniscule, is significant in shaping your existence. Believe that this is true and prepare to meet your mate. I will show you the way.

Believing in yourself and in a power greater than you will lead you to your beloved. Have faith, and prepare yourself for an amazing journey.

Your Journey Begins

The notion of soulmates stems from the concepts of reincarnation and karma. You and your soulmate have been together before. Your souls now desire a reconnection.

Therefore, before we go any further I will give a brief but practical explanation of these subjects to help you understand why we attract certain people into our lives. Now, remember that you can benefit from the information in this book whether or not you believe in reincarnation, or spiritualism for that matter. While a strong belief in the spiritual aspects of this book is not necessary for a belief in soulmates, an open mind and an open heart are essential.

You Have Been Here Before

Reincarnation is the doctrine that says that we evolve spiritually by living as many lifetimes as is necessary to achieve perfection.
— Richard Webster

All life exists on two basic planes: the physical, where we live with our physical bodies, and the spiritual, which we refer to as heaven. When our physical body dies, our soul travels to the spiritual plane, and stays there until we are ready to begin our new life. We keep coming back to the physical plane lifetime after lifetime to resolve our issues and gain greater wisdom and enlightenment.

Some people are sceptical about the concept of reincarnation, but it is steadily becoming much more accepted. Numerous people believe that their souls are immortal and that when they are born, their souls brings with them all the wisdom, knowledge, and karma they have gained from previous lives.

We must all work though hardships, challenges, and difficulties. Life on the physical plane is a series of learning experiences through which we, along with others we have known in past lives, work out our past karma. This advances us towards a higher state of awareness.

Reincarnation experts believe that when we are souls in the spiritual world, full of wisdom and light, we create our own new life. We decide, along with our guardians and spiritual masters, what we need to accomplish, what lessons we need to learn, and how and with whom we will balance our karma. Many believe that we choose our sex and our culture, as well as our parents, siblings, close friends, and soulmates. We choose to reincarnate with these people because we share a strong bond and because they will provide us with the opportunity to balance past karma and subsequently evolve spiritually.

We choose the occurrences that are essential for us to experience in our lifetime in order to begin our spiritual revolution. We chose to reincarnate so we can learn lessons, balance our karma, and fulfill the destiny that will advance us on our spiritual pathway. We live as many lives as we need to achieve perfection. The only thing we do not choose is the outcome of our experiences here on earth; our free will determines this, depending upon our present circumstances (more on free will in the next section).

A soul family is made up of people with whom we are very closely bonded and choose to work for many lifetimes. Our soulmates are not all romantic partners (although this is the focus of this book). They are our spiritual family. They can be children, treasured friends, or family members. Physical families tend to incarnate in groups. Soulmates can be of the opposite or the same sex. Romantic soulmate relationships are not restricted to heterosexual relationships either.

These kindred spirits are not necessarily with you throughout your entire life. However long they stay, they will impact your life in some way. Many will come for short periods of time just to help you achieve a goal or to set you on the right path. Whatever the reason, they are in your life to help you grow as a person or to be a source of support for you. All of our relationships will provide us with opportunities for learning.

So, we now know that our soulmates are people with whom we share a strong spiritual bond that has existed through many reincarnations.

Before we reincarnate, we make plans to meet our soulmates at certain times in our lives that will be right for both of us. We come into this world knowing all this, but at some point in our voyage from the spirit world to the physical one we forget. However, all is not lost. All our past experiences are stored in our subconscious minds and our souls remember.

Free Will Is Our Birthright

Some people are disturbed by the fact that our lives are fated; they fear that they have no control over their lives. However, nothing could be further from the truth. We have all been blessed with the gift of free will and nothing is fully predestined.

While I strongly believe in destiny and fate, I also believe that they exist side by side with free will. We are all masters of our destiny, co-creating with Spirit. We are in control of our lives and we have complete freedom to fulfill (or not fulfill) that which we came here to experience and discover. Fate will make sure that we get the *opportunity* to fulfill our destiny, but it is up to us whether we choose to rise to the occasion or not.

For example, let's say that you meet your soulmate. You feel the strong connection that everyone talks about and you cannot stop thinking about this person who has been brought into your life. Unfortunately, however, you have a commitment to someone else and it would be irresponsible of you to break it. Perhaps there are children involved and ending your relationship would not be fair to them. (This is the reason I advise singles not to rush into a committed relationship or a marriage if they are not sure that they are with their loving soulmate.) Or perhaps your soulmate exercise his or her free will and chooses not to be with you (for whatever reason), even though you made plans in the spirit world to be together.

As you can see from these examples, your present circumstances determine whether or not you choose to be together and your free will allows you to make decisions and control your own destiny.

What Is Karma and How Does It Affect Us?

Karma is the law of cause and effect, which means that for every effect, there must be a cause. The legendary cliché states, "What goes around comes around." Our actions from this life and past lives need to be balanced. The golden rule, "Do onto others as you would have them do unto you," is the underlying principle of karma.

Karma can be either positive or negative. We produce good karma when we are positive, compassionate, thoughtful, or kind. The opposite is also true. If we think or act in an irresponsible, selfish, greedy, thoughtless, revengeful, or mean-spirited way, we produce negative karma, which we will have to deal with in the future. Keep in mind that we have to earn what we receive.

We create our own karma by the way in which we lead our lives. How we are treated in this life is a direct reflection of how we treated others in the past. The way in which we live now will directly impact the quality of this life and the next. We have the opportunity to set the balance right again.

We should not fear karma, since it exists not to make us miserable or to punish us, but rather to help us learn and grow towards a state of perfection and wisdom. We become undivided and complete people when we are balanced in body, mind, and spirit. We created the experiences in our lives that allow us to balance our karma.

Everything in life happens for a reason, and there are no coincidences. It is really very simple: if we do not learn our lessons, we have no choice but to repeat them, either in this life or the next.

Three Types of Soulmates

There are many different views on what a soulmate is and on what these relationships are all about. Some of my views might differ from those of others who write or speak about this subject. After conversations with many enlightened individuals, my personal experiences and observations, and years of research, I have come to realize that there are three different types of soulmate relationships: Twin Flame, loving, and karmic.

I trust that an understanding of the unique characteristics of these types of soulmates as well as of the tasks they come into our lives to fulfill will help you to recognize your own soulmates. This will allow you to make an educated decision as to whether you want to go through the sometimes heartbreaking experience of a karmic soulmate relationship or a joyful one with your loving soulmate.

So let's get started.

Twin Flames: Our One and Only

Two souls with but a single thought, two hearts that beat as one.

— Unknown

Because there are many theories among spiritual experts regarding Twin Flame relationships (sometimes referred to as Twin Souls), the subject can be confusing and difficult to comprehend. However, most agree that our Twin Soul is our one and only "true soulmate." It has been said that Twin Souls share the same soul.

The belief that we all have a Twin Soul has existed for thousands of years. The great Greek philosopher Plato described a person's Twin Soul as the "actual half of himself." Plato explains, "The pair is lost in an amazement of love and friendship and intimacy and one will not be out of the other's sight."

In his book entitled *Love and Sexuality*, Omraam Mikhael Aivanhov states, "When man leapt like a spark from the bosom of his Creator he was two in one, and these two parts complemented each other perfectly, each was the other's twin." According to Aivanhov, at some point these two halves separate and go in different directions, and each evolves separately. Only after many incarnations, during which each half lives up to its true spiritual essence, can the Twin Souls reunite.

We do not necessarily get to be with our Twin Souls in each lifetime. Nevertheless, even when we are not together we are still working, consciously or unconsciously, towards being together by balancing our karma and evolving spiritually. Our souls never forget that they are incomplete without our Twin Souls. They are always searching for their missing half. Only when we have reached this balance can we be together.

We share a deep spiritual bond with these souls. We are physically, spiritually, mentally, and emotionally compatible and we complete and balance each other perfectly. This eternal love is truly a relationship made in heaven, and the spiritual love Twin Souls share is amazing.

As you may have guessed, these relationships are rare, the domain of only a few very enlightened souls. Some believe that Twin Souls are brought together on earth to fulfill a great mission of service to others.

If you wish to learn more about Twin Souls, I have listed some titles in the recommended reading section at the back of this book.

Loving Soulmates: Your Special Someone

Thomas Moore, a psychotherapist, writer, and lecturer, describes a soulmate as "someone to whom we feel profoundly connected, as though the communication and communing that takes place between us were not the product of intentional efforts, but rather a divine grace. This kind of relationship is so important to the soul that many have said there is nothing more precious in life."

Soulmates (sometimes referred to as *kindred spirits*) are the special people in our lives with whom we are compatible and very connected in this lifetime. Our loving soulmates are nurturing and kind, and they give us all the love and support we need without asking for anything in return. Their love is beyond measure and they accept us and love us as we are. When we meet a loving soulmate, we share an immediate trust, as well as our most intimate feelings and thoughts with them.

We are content and completely at ease and fulfilled when we are together. And, of course, the experience is mutual.

We are strongly linked to our spiritual partners because we are familiar souls and have shared many lives together. We share a common path as well as a common life purpose. We have similar life lessons to learn. We complement each other's masculine and feminine traits and balance each other fully.

When you reunite with your loving soulmate, the feelings are entirely different than what you have experienced in a normal or karmic relationship (see below). A loving soulmate relationship feels like you have reunited with someone you have known for a very long time. If you and your soulmate are ready for this relationship, an immediate and profound connection will be felt and an intense and heavenly union will ignite. You will feel totally at peace and at ease with this person. You will enjoy being together and will help each other become better people. You and your true love have shared many positive past lives and have come together in this life to enjoy each other again and to continue your journey. This new life will bring many new opportunities to deepen your love even more.

We are rewarded with these types of relationships when we have learned our lessons from past karmic relationships and when we are emotionally mature and ready for our partnership.

Do We Have More than One Loving Soulmate?

When most of us speak of soulmates, we think of one special individual with whom we will fall madly in love with and live happily ever after. Bombarded with glamorous images from the media and Hollywood, many of us search endlessly for this one true love. But the truth is that we can have a soulmate connection with a number of people.

It is important to keep in mind that your one and only soulmate is your Twin Soul. These relationships are rare and we are not blessed with them in each lifetime. In fact, many spiritual experts believe that our Twin Soul may not even have incarnated in this lifetime. There is a good chance that your Twin Soul is with you only in spirit, guiding you and helping you from other realms.

So do we have more than one loving soulmate? Yes, nearly everyone does. Considering that we live many lives, it only makes sense that we would have several soulmates with whom we are compatible. So if you have lost a soulmate relationship in the past—whether through death, a break-up, or divorce—you can rest assured that you will get another chance.

Some people who have lost a soulmate doubt the fact that they were soulmates or the importance of that relationship. They say things like "We must not have been soulmates or he/she would never have left me." But time has nothing to do with the quality of soulmate relationships. Whether they last three months or three years, they can still be good for us.

Soulmates come into our lives for a purpose. They teach us something about ourselves or to clarify something for us so we can move forward. Soulmates usually leave our lives when the lessons that we came together to learn are complete. Loving us unconditionally, they may leave to make room for an even higher quality soulmate relationship to enter our life. In other cases they leave for only a short while, because we may grow more by not being in a relationship at that time. Over time, several soulmates may take us, step by step, to meet our ideal soulmates.

I have found in the course of my research for this book that those who have experienced a soulmate relationship but have lost it almost always have another. So please don't settle for just anybody in order to have someone with whom to share your life. Your soulmate may come back into your life, as Amy's story demonstrates.

Amy's Story

I was only 18 years of age when I met John. He was my first real love. Our relationship was fulfilling and happy and we loved each other very much. But after two and a half years, I started to get restless. I felt like I was missing out. My friends were having a great time dating different people and I wanted to experience different relationships as well.

One day I told John how I felt. Although he was very hurt, he said he understood. He believed that if we were meant to be together, we would meet again in the future.

John and I went our separate ways. He accepted a job out of town and we lost touch. I dated several men and was in and out of relationships for the next five years. Although many of those men were wonderful, I could not find what I had experienced with John. Not a day went by that I did not think of him.

After a few years apart, I began to have vivid dreams of us being together again. I would wake up very disappointed when I realized that they were only dreams. As the years dragged on, I started to really miss him and wish we were together again. I wondered where he was and if he were married. I often thought of his last words to me so long ago, "If we're meant to be, we will meet again."

One evening at a party, much to my surprise, I noticed John chatting with some friends. My heart started racing and my palms began to sweat. I couldn't believe my eyes. Was it really him? I noticed that he wasn't with anyone which made me extremely happy. As I was trying to calm myself down, John walked towards me. Our eyes met and without saying a word we fell into each other's arms in the warmest and longest hug I have ever experienced. It all felt so familiar, and so right. We just seemed to fit in each other's arms so well, as if we were made for each other. At that moment we both knew that we were soulmates and meant to be together. I feel so blessed to have been given a second chance. I will never take our love for granted again.

It is evident that when Amy first went out with John, she was not mature or confident enough to know that he really was her loving soulmate. She had to experience other relationships to appreciate what she had with John. Once she did come to this important realization, her desire to get him back brought him into her life once again, when they were both free and ready for the relationship.

Karmic Relationships

Maybe God wants us to meet a few wrong people before meeting the right one so that when we finally meet the right person, we will know to be grateful for that gift.
— Unknown

What Is a Karmic Soulmate?
Karmic soulmates are drawn together to balance a spiritual debt and sometimes-negative mutual karma, which is most likely from a past life. Karmic soulmates experience a strong sense of connection—either attraction or an intense dislike. In the latter case, it could be that their experience together in a past lifetime was difficult or traumatic.

Because of the intense feelings they generate, karmic soulmates are often mistaken for the real thing (loving soulmates). However, there is a clear distinction between the two. Loving soulmate relationships are harmonious, warm, and provide feelings of comfort and safety, while karmic relationships are generally unhealthy and dysfunctional. They can be intense and difficult, leaving their participants physically and emotionally exhausted.

Most of us have been involved in karmic relationships at some point and the majority of marriages that fail are karmic marriages. These types of relationships are commonly one-sided or unbalanced. One partner seems to be giving more to the relationship while the other takes and gives little back in return. This type of love does not always make sense to the rest of the world or even to the individuals involved. Although those in karmic relationships will probably never feel completely fulfilled and satisfied, they often cannot help the strong love/hate union that they have with their partner.

Regrettably, some individuals attract karmic relationships over and over. This is because they have established a negative pattern for themselves—either in this life or in past lives—which needs to be broken, or they have not learned the lessons that these relationships are meant to provide them. Remember that all relationships are destined to be repeated until their lessons are learned and you are healed. These lessons are meant to prepare you to move on to a more loving soulmate relationship and until you learn them, you will continue to choose unsuitable partners.

Karmic relationships are not inevitable. You can, and most of the time should, avoid them. Your intuition will always try to warn you against getting involved in karmic relationships especially at the beginning stages. You will get plenty of warning signs (more on these in Chapter 6), so pay close attention. If you are familiar with the different kinds of relationships, you can recognize them and decide whether you want to take the sometimes strenuous, painful path of a karmic relationship or a more balanced, enjoyable one with your loving soulmate.

It is a commonly accepted adage that wisdom erases karma. If you are in a karmic relationship, you don't have to continue to suffer. You can free yourself of the karma that you have acquired with this person by learning what you need to learn from the relationship. Usually the lesson is as simple as admitting to yourself that you deserve better and valuing yourself enough to end it.

You can break the karmic pattern by avoiding these connections and choosing healthier, more secure partnerships. Remember that we have been given free will. Nothing is so fated that it cannot be changed. We do have a choice of whom we want to be with and of which path to follow.

Although karmic relationships can be exhilarating and passionate, most of them do not last. Once your karma with your partner is complete, you will find the courage to move on because the relationship will no longer have the energy it had before you learned your lesson. These relationships do serve a purpose: we learn our greatest lessons through them. View them not as failures, but as stepping-stones to the loving soulmate connection that awaits you.

Karmic Marriages

If you are married to someone whom you know is not your loving soulmate, please do not panic. Many people are in the same situation. For some, it is not in their destiny to be with their loving soulmate in this lifetime. Perhaps they need to experience a karmic partnership in order to balance some past karma.

Experts believe that although karmic marriages can be very difficult at times, it is entirely possible for them to be fulfilling. Elizabeth Clare Prophet, spiritual expert and author of *Soul Mates and Twin Flames*, explains, "These marriages are often difficult, but they are important in achieving mastery on the spiritual path. The husband and wife also gain the good karma of sponsoring and nurturing their children." We will be with our true soulmates again in the spirit world and in many lifetimes to come. Therefore, make the best of your present circumstances and you will be rewarded. Any relationship that is based on mutual affection, consideration, respect, and understanding can be made to work, but only if that is what both partners are striving for. It is also entirely possible, through hard work, commitment, and plenty of communication, to turn your karmic relationship into an affectionate soulmate relationship. The key ingredient, of course is unconditional, unselfish love.

I strongly believe that if you have made a serious commitment, such as marriage, then you should do everything in your power to save that relationship. Never use the soulmate theory to walk away from your commitment to your spouse. Honour your commitment to this person. If the marriage is in trouble, do not be afraid to seek professional help from a therapist or counsellor.

However, if the relationship is abusive in any way then I advise you to get out. There are three types of abuse:

1. *Verbal*—name-calling like "ugly," "fat," "insane," "whore," "stupid," or "loser"
2. *Emotional*—intimidation, manipulation, belittling, threatening to leave you, and trying to scare you
3. *Physical*—hitting, pushing, throwing things

Many people are in denial about emotional and verbal abuse. They believe that just because their partner is not physically hitting them, then they are not being abused. These people minimize the severity of the problem and make excuses for the abuser's behaviour, such as "She is under a lot of stress," or "He had a bad day at work." What these people fail to realize is that verbal and emotional abuse is devastating. It eats at your self-esteem and sense of self-worth and the scars can be deeper and much longer lasting than physical ones. Every time you allow someone to disrespect you, tear you down, or belittle you, you allow him or her to take a little piece of your self-confidence, until you have none left. Your spirit will eventually be crushed, and no relationship is worth that. You deserve better.

Now that we know about the unique characteristics of different types of soulmates, it is time to learn some relationship skills so we can avoid karmic connections that bring us down. The rest of this book is about what we need to do to prepare to meet the right soulmate. I will also discuss how, when, and where we can reunite with our spiritual partners and what we need to do to keep our loved ones in our lives once they've arrived. Read on; the best is yet to come.

At that moment, it seemed to him that time stood still, and the Soul of the World surged within him. When he looked into her dark eyes . . . he learned the most important part of the language that all the world spoke—the language that everyone on earth was capable of understanding in their heart. It was love. . . . It required no explanation, just as the universe needs none as it travels through endless time. What the boy felt at that moment he was in the presence of the only woman in his life, and that, with no need for words, she recognized the same thing.

— Paulo Coelho, *The Alchemist*

CHAPTER 2
AVOIDING RELATIONSHIPS THAT BRING YOU DOWN

If you are a passive person who needs to be part of a couple in order to feel good about yourself, then you are not ready to meet your loving soulmate. You need to do some work on yourself first. If you get involved in obsessive karmic relationships over and over, this chapter will help you identify this, so you can make healthier love choices in the future. In this chapter I will show you how you can take control of your life and take your power back.

Obsessive Love: The Wrong Kind of Love

Obsessive love is usually karmic love. It is often mistaken for soulmate love because of the strong feelings it involves. However, obsessive love is needy, controlling, and sometimes even abusive. People tend to get involved in these relationships when they are feeling lonely. Deep down inside these people believe they don't deserve quality love.

Obsessive love is a compulsive behaviour; it is not real love. We all experience infatuation, lust, dependency, and possessiveness at some point, but they should not be mistaken for real love. Real love involves trust, respect, and admiration for one another.

People who are addicted to love are obsessed with taking care of another person, to the point that they neglect to care for or value themselves. They make immense sacrifices for their partner and their relationship. They do whatever it takes to hang on to their partner, even if it means giving up time with other loved ones. They often experience extreme mood swings and deny any problems in their relationship, not only to friends and family, but also to themselves.

They may cover up their partner's faults and even lie for them. They take on their partner's personality, likes, and dislikes, and lose their identity and self-esteem in the process. They may also adopt their partner's bad habits and jeopardize their own health. Although they may seem self-reliant to the rest of the world, when it comes down to love, they lose themselves.

While those obsessed with love come from all different ages, cultures, and financial backgrounds, women have a tendency to lose themselves in relationships more so than men. They often attract tough-guy types and think they're in love too quickly. Experts say that those obsessed with love did not develop a sense of themselves early in life, making them unable to handle love relationships. They are not clear about their goals, values, or what they truly want out of life and their relationships. They have a difficult time standing up for themselves and tend to choose partners who are controlling and even abusive. The more mistreatment these individuals endure, the more they try to please. .

If you recognize this behaviour in yourself, you must take the necessary steps to change it. Never stay in a relationship that is unhealthy, controlling, or abusive. It will eventually take its toll on you, perhaps leading to poor health and destructive behaviours.

The first step to healing is to admit that you have a problem. While you shouldn't feel bad about past mistakes, you cannot deny them either. Instead, look on them not as mistakes, but as learning experiences.

Being aware of the problem is half the battle. There are lessons to learn in these relationships; until you learn them and release the experience you will continue to relive them over and over again. All that is usually required is a change in attitude. Make this change and look forward to a bright new future.

Nancy's Story

I met Steven at a nightclub while celebrating my 23rd birthday with my two best friends. He was good looking, in a macho kind of way—just the type of guy I usually go for. Although Steven was a little rough around the edges and could be a little rude, I found myself extremely attracted to him.

Steven and I started dating. Our relationship was like a rollercoaster right from the start. One minute we'd be fighting and the next we would be making passionate love. Although Steven could be absolutely wonderful at times, he could also be moody, angry, and controlling—a real jerk. I threatened to leave him on numerous occasions but I couldn't muster up the courage to do so.

My friends and family were convinced that this guy was not for me, but I just couldn't bear the thought of leaving him. He needed me and I needed him too much to leave. However, after three very long years, I finally realized that I was no longer the happy-go-lucky girl I once was. I was exhausted emotionally and physically and my self-esteem was at an all-time low. I had to do something to get my old life back if I ever wanted to be happy again. I had to find the courage within myself to end my relationship with Steven once and for all and make a fresh start.

One evening when Steven was in one of his bad moods, blaming me for everything that was wrong with our relationship, I finally had enough. I got the nerve to leave him and I never looked back. It was the most liberating experience of my life.

About six months later I met John at a work-related seminar. We hit it off right away and started dating. The more time we spent together, the stronger our bond became. I have never felt this way about anyone before. We both want the same things out of life and our value systems are the same.

I know without a shadow of a doubt that I have met "the one." It just all feels so right. John and I plan to be married within a year.

As you can see from Nancy's story, she rushed into her relationship with Steven. What she felt for him was primarily a physical attraction and she ran with it. She ignored the warning signs right, such as his rudeness. To top it off, her friends warned her, but did she listen? *No!* Nancy felt flattered that this good-looking, tough guy showed an interest in her and she did not consider whether or not he was right for her. She did not think about the fact that they were poles apart and had different value systems. This relationship was doomed from the start.

Obsessive relationships are addicting, which is why Nancy should be complimented. She loved herself enough and showed enough courage to get out of this karmic and obsessive relationship before she got in even deeper or it led to marriage. If she hadn't, she would have missed out on the soulmate relationship with John that was waiting for her.

Remember, your true love (loving soulmate) would not mistreat you, control your every move, take advantage of you, or ask you to sacrifice your interests, values, friends, or family. He or she would love you as you are, respect your values, and encourage the relationships that are important to you because he or she wants you to be happy.

When Your Partner Won't Commit

Are you in love with a person who has never expressed any interest in getting married? If you intend to be married, then it is important that you don't waste precious time on relationships that are going nowhere. If you are of a reasonable age (25 and older), you've been with someone you truly love for a long time (over two years), and he or she is not committing to you by setting a wedding date, then it's time to put a little pressure on. Although you should never manipulate anyone into marrying you, you need to know where you stand and what your partner's intentions are. Discussing marriage is important so that there are no misunderstandings that can delay your plan to marry.

Mary's Story

Mary is 28 years old and has been in a live-in relationship with Robert, who is 34, for four years. Since she was a young girl, Mary dreamed of being married by 25 and having children right away.

For the past year or so, Mary had been wondering if Robert would ever propose. With a little pressure from her best friend, she finally mustered up enough nerve to approach the subject with Robert. Mary was very surprised when Robert told her in no uncertain terms that he never had any intention of marrying her or anyone else. "Why," she asked, "didn't you tell me earlier?" He answered, "You never asked."

This is why it is so important to ask the right questions.

The signs of and reasons behind a fear of commitment are discussed in more detail in Chapter 6. However, be aware that to a lot of men (and some women) the "C" word means a loss of freedom and privacy, and the thought of committing to monogamy or marriage is not a pleasant one.

You must make it clear to your partner what your goals are and what you want. Try not to be needy; allow your partner time to think about it without too much pressure. If your partner does not commit to you by setting a wedding date within a few months after the talk, then you're probably not with your soulmate.

Sylvia's Story

I have been dating Anthony exclusively for almost five years. And although we have had the commitment talk many times in the past, he still has not proposed marriage.

When I question Anthony's intentions he always says all the right things, like how much he loves me, how he will marry me some day, and on and on. He says he just needs more time to get his life together and save more money before he can commit to a marriage.

I have been hearing these words for many years now. We both have good jobs and we both make decent money, so when he uses money as a reason not to commit to me, I wonder if he is just stringing me along.

My family is convinced that Anthony is not serious about marrying me and that I am being used. Anthony and I have had our share of problems, but I do love him. I have been with him for so long that I can't see my life without him and the thought of starting over is real scary.

Sylvia's story is not unusual. Unfortunately, some people want all the benefits of a relationship without the commitment. They will keep promising to marry you someday, but that day may never come. And they won't release you either, probably because they don't want someone else to have you.

Don't believe the overused excuses about needing to be financially secure or to find themselves first. Be aware that you are being deceived. Read between the lines. A person who won't commit to you does not truly love you and is not your loving soulmate. It's that simple.

It is extremely important that life partners have an honest relationship. When they deceive each other by being dishonest or giving empty promises, they are robbing their partners of their most prized possessions: their self-esteem and time. The negative karma they are creating for themselves will, sooner or later, need to be balanced.

Just Love Is Not Enough

Many of us jump in and out of relationships with the wrong people and would not be able to recognize true love even if it were staring us in the face. We squander our time, energy, and emotions on relationships that are clearly unsuitable for us. Choosing our life partner is one of the most important decisions we will make during our lifetime. Some of us, however, are not taking this decision seriously enough.

"But I love him!" I cannot tell you how many times I've heard this. While love certainly can help you get through some tough times, in itself it is not enough. Just because you love someone does not mean that he or she is the right partner for you. Nor does it mean that you should marry him or her, or put up with unacceptable behaviour. Sometimes we can love someone and still not be a good match.

Real life is not like the movies. Love does not conquer all. In the real world differing belief systems and values (about family, kids, money, long-term goals, etc.) can cause major problems in a relationship. We need to choose our partners with more care if we want to be happy and fulfilled in our lives.

Don't enter into a relationship thinking you can change your partner. You must be absolutely sure that you truly adore this person as he or she is, and that you share values and similar desires. Ask yourself whether this person is the one with whom you want to spend the rest of your life, whether you want the same things out of life, or whether this relationship is really just another learning experience.

If the latter, then it is in your best interests to move on. If you wait until you fall completely out of love with this person, you could be waiting a long time. Remember that you will always have feelings for someone with whom you have shared so much of yourself, but this is no reason to stick around if you are unhappy.

I asked my friend Maria why she married her now ex-husband whom, she confided in me, she was not passionate about to begin with. This is her answer: "I knew that we were very different and had nothing in common. I had doubts about the relationship from the start, but then he would say he loved me so much that he couldn't imagine his life without me in it. That was it. He had me. I couldn't resist after those words. He just loved me so much."

Unfortunately, this is a common response among people who are in love with love. They have such a strong need to be loved that they place little importance on whether they are in love with this person or whether this person is right for them.

If you are in love with someone you know is not good for you and you are not happy and fulfilled in the relationship, then I'm afraid I need to advise you to move on. It will be extremely hard and take a lot of courage, especially if you have been together for a long time. However, it will be the smartest thing you ever do.

A MATTER OF DESTINY

Sometimes we want to be in love so badly that we convince ourselves that we are with our soulmate. And, all too frequently, we make the mistake of marrying someone before we know the difference between infatuation and real love, something that we cannot truly understand until we've met our true love. Until then, we just aren't familiar with that special energy and bond that only spiritual loving soulmates naturally share.

Loving Others without Losing Ourselves

People obsessed with love tend to be overly accommodating to their partners. They think that they have to earn their partner's love. They cater to their every desire, for fear of losing their partner.

These individuals are fighting a losing battle. Catering to your partner only makes you seem needy; instead of loving you more, he or she will respect you less, will stop romancing you, and will treat you more like a servant then a partner. Your behaviour is a sign of insecurity, and insecurity is not an attractive trait. Putting others before your own needs and well-being tells them that you don't think highly of yourself.

A relationship is a matter of give and take. If you keep on giving and your partner continues to take, you will end up feeling used and taken for granted, eventually resenting your partner. It is important to set boundaries.

I don't mean to imply that you should never do nice things for your loved ones, but your generosity should be reciprocated and appreciated. Being a nice person means being considerate, respectful, and honest, but it doesn't mean you have to be anyone's servant. Realize your worth and allow your partner to do nice things for you too.

JOANNE B. PARROTTA

Change Is Difficult

When one door of happiness closes, another opens; but often we look so long at the closed door that we do not see the one which has been opened for us.
— Helen Keller

Change is extremely difficult and sometimes scary for someone who is obsessed with love. A relationship may be unfulfilling and unhappy, but it is still familiar territory. Let's face it: we're all a little afraid of being lonely.

Many people do not want to face the fact that their relationship is not working. They don't want it to end, maybe because they think there's no one better out there for them. Perhaps they want to get married and start a family and the thought of starting over with someone new scary. Maybe they just don't want to hurt the person they're with. Or maybe this person is good marriage material and can provide them with the security they need and want.

These are all wrong reasons to stay in a relationship. When a relationship is not going the way you'd hoped and you are no longer happy, you must do what's right for you. When it comes to choosing a life partner, you are allowed to be selfish; you must put your own needs first.

If you are contemplating ending a relationship, first ask yourself the following questions:

1. Is my partner in love with me? And, am I in love with him or her?
2. Am I happy with our life together?
3. Does he or she treat me with respect?
4. Does my partner keep his or her promises?

5. Is my partner honest and faithful?
6. Do my family and friends like my partner?
7. Will my partner make a good parent someday?
8. Does my partner make me one of his or her first priorities?

If the answers to these questions make it clear that this relationship is not right for you, honour your feelings. Let this person go with love, but let them go. Free yourself and your partner so that your true loves have the chance to come into both your lives.

Ending a long-term relationship can be very difficult and this may be a trying time for you. Mourn the loss by taking time out from romantic relationships. Then wipe those tears away and work on being the best you can be: concentrate on your family and friends, set your house in order, tend to business, get clear on what you want and need in your life and relationships, and wait on destiny to make it happen.

Finding the Courage to Let Go

When we turn to our Higher Power in trust, we can say good-by to the relationship, knowing its ending is for the best. Letting go of our pain frees us to accept the new joys God has in store for us.
— Letting Go, *Meditations for Codependents*

When we let go of something or someone who no longer makes us happy, we open the door to receive something new and better. The universe does not open this door until we let go of what we're holding on to. The longer we wait, the harder it gets, so the time to make a decision and take a leap of faith is *now*.

Think of it this way: the fact that you're not fulfilled and happy and that you're experiencing problems in your current relationship is also part of fate. It's your soul trying to tell you to free yourself so your meant-to-be love can enter your life.

Unfortunately some relationships are meant to be difficult. Think of them not as mistakes, but as a learning experience for both of you. Learn the lessons that you are meant to learn, or you will continue to encounter difficult relationships until you finally get it. Work to resolve the issues as quickly as possible so that you can move into a kinder, more loving relationship.

You are entitled to happiness; just love isn't enough. Ending a relationship may feel like the end of the world, but you will soon realize that it's really the beginning of a whole new world. Embrace it and remember that for every ending there is a beginning—that's cosmic law. Every relationship and every event happens in order to push you towards your next phase of life and to help you grow as a person.

A Wake-Up Call

If we resist change, or if we are in denial about the issues we are meant to work through in this life, the universe will have no choice but to give us a wake-up call. This wake-up call is also known as the universal kick in the behind. It can come in the form of an unexpected job loss or the loss of a relationship that is not for your highest good and was not meant to be. Do not view it as a negative thing, but rather as a necessary step to get you moving towards your chosen path.

As I am writing this, a perfect example comes to mind. One day not too long ago, as I was having my morning coffee at work, a co-worker and friend named Sandra joined me in the lunchroom. I could tell by the look on her face that something was on her mind, and I intuitively picked up that it had to do with her boyfriend.

Sandra's Story

Sandra has been in a very unhealthy relationship for the past three years with a man named Robert. Friends and family had pleaded with her to end this relationship, but she refused to listen to anyone. She claimed that she loved him and could not see herself with anyone else but him. It has been extremely hard to watch this beautiful, intelligent woman's self-esteem, health, and happiness deteriorate because of this relationship.

As she sat down, she told me that a couple of days earlier, while walking home from work, she saw Robert in the arms of another woman. To make matters worse, this woman was a mutual friend. When she confronted him that evening, he told her that he had been having an affair for six months, and that he no longer wanted to be with her.

She was devastated, but, although it broke my heart to see her so miserable, I knew that this was actually a blessing in disguise. Sandra had held onto this relationship for longer than she should have. Her self-esteem was so low that she did not have the strength to let go on her own, but was forced to get out of it by a power greater than she, who had her best interest at heart. She had received a wake-up call.

The universe, God, her Twin Soul, angels, or whatever you want to call it intervened on Sandra's behalf and provided that wake-up call she so desperately needed to get on with her life. We must remember that if we resist changing and growing, we will be forced to change and grow.

JOANNE B. PARROTTA

Confidence Is Beautiful

If we feel empty without a soulmate, we will be just as empty with one.
— Marian Young Starnes

It's time to stop giving too much of yourself in relationships and to start working on building your self-esteem. The more you love yourself, the more people will respect you and the less they will mistreat you. People take advantage only of those who let them, so don't let them. Remember that whatever you are willing to put up with is exactly what you will receive.

No one can take your power unless you give it away, so demand to be treated with love and respect. Say what you want, think, and feel. Make your own choices, and learn to say no when appropriate. Let others know where you stand right from the start and you will get the respect you deserve. Value yourself enough to please yourself first. This is what will draw in the highest and best soulmate.

Do some soul-searching in order to get to know yourself and find out what type of person you would really like to be with before you jump into your next relationship. It is necessary that we know who we are before we can truly share our lives with someone else. Getting into and out of unhealthy relationships can only make us very unhappy.

A self-reliant, independent person knows that a loving relationship is just the icing, not the whole cake. It is very important to keep our own identity, interests, and friends, and we mustn't get so caught up in our partner's life that we forget to take care of our own needs and those of our loved ones. We must also be able to face our own problems. Finding a partner will not make them magically disappear, leaving us with only happiness. We must find ourselves first; then and only then will true love come into view.

The next part of this book will help you prepare yourself in body, mind, and spirit, so you can attract the right relationship.

When you know {the Universal Language of the World}, it's easy to understand that someone in the world awaits you, whether it's in the middle of the desert or in some great city. And when two such people encounter each other, and their eyes meet, the past and the future become unimportant. There is only that moment, and the incredible certainty that everything under the sun has been written by one hand only. It is the hand that evokes love, and creates a twin soul for every person in the world. Without such love, one's dreams would have no meaning.

— Paulo Coelho, *The Alchemist*

CHAPTER 3
PREPARING TO MEET YOUR LOVING SOULMATE

Now that you know what to look for in a relationship and what to avoid, it is time to prepare yourself so you can meet your chosen one. To stop attracting karmic mates, you need to become the kind of person to whom your loving soulmate would be drawn. Your loving soulmate could not possibly be attracted to someone who did not love him or herself.

When we seek a soulmate, we are seeking a higher quality of love. The more we elevate our own vibration, the better our chances of attracting this kind of love. When we connect with our loving soulmate, we have, in effect, found a mate for where we are in our development as a soul. By working on the imperfections from within and making the switch to a happier, healthier lifestyle, you will increase your self-confidence. By developing a relationship with yourself, you will be ready to receive healthy love.

Doing the Inner Work

A correct relationship with oneself is of primary importance, for from it flows all possible right relationships with others. When we change our attitude from negative to positive, it jump-starts new energy, allowing us to enter into a state of heightened awareness.

To attract a high-quality soulmate, you must attain a high-quality personality of your very own. Become a veritable magnet for your soulmate by getting in touch with your feelings, looking deep to see what you are inside, and doing the work necessary to become a fully loving and vibrantly alive person. By renewing your interest in life, you start things moving. You rarely get more from life than what you feel worthy of receiving. Set your goals and always expect a positive outcome.

You don't have to be perfect, especially good-looking, or highly intelligent to experience this true love. These relationships do not happen to just a lucky few; they can happen to you. But you have to do your inner work first. Start by loving and taking care of yourself and then work on building your self-esteem and healing your heart. Start filling your life with the people and the things you love. Clear all that negative energy and toxic thinking. Then take the risk, and go for your dreams.

Letting Go of the Past

We all walk through life with emotional baggage. But when we dwell on past hurts, we can't focus on the present. Now is the time to let go of the past, to release that which no longer serves your growth, and to rebuild upon a new foundation. The past is gone; no amount of worrying or thinking can change that. Say goodbye to it, thanking all the experiences for the lessons they have brought you.

As you let go of the past, free yourself from the need to punish and be punished and release any guilt you may be carrying around unnecessarily. It is time to stop being a victim and to take responsibility for your own life. Release emotional disappointments, abandonment issues, bad romantic relationships, and negative beliefs.

A MATTER OF DESTINY

Forgiveness is the first step towards real peace and happiness and plays a major part in allowing love into your life. Being unforgiving is a toxin we store in our bodies. It is now time to release that toxic energy. Forgive yourself in order to forgive others. This will allow you to let go, once and for all, of your emotional baggage.

Forgive yourself, your ex, your parents, and anyone else who has ever hurt you. I am not asking you to condone what any of these people have done to you. You are not doing this for them at all; you are doing it for yourself. Let it go and move on.

Identify and heal any unhealthy emotional patterns from the past so you don't sabotage your future relationships. Universal law states that like attracts like. If worry, fear, depression, doubt, or desperation is the energy you generate, then you'll magnetize depressed or wounded people. Just by acknowledging that you have some emotional baggage and are willing to release it, you are well on your way to healing.

One of the reasons why a lot of people are not with their spiritual partners is that they consciously or unconsciously believe that something as special as a soulmate relationship is not possible for them. Deep inside they really believe that they do not deserve this high-quality love. Ask yourself the following questions:

1. Do you believe there is no loving soulmate for you?
2. Do you believe that soulmates are just a myth?
3. Have you given up looking for your ideal mate?

If you answered *yes*, you must shift your attitude before you can locate your mate. You must get rid of this negativity; you are literally scaring away potential mates from entering your life.

Don't allow hurts from past relationships to hinder you from finding your special someone. All your past relationships—yes, even the bad ones—served a purpose towards your self-growth. Now it's time to move on.

Let Go of the Fear

After being hurt in the past, you may feel unwilling to risk disappointment. You may have had your heart broken many times and have closed yourself off to avoid further hurt. But did you ever stop and think that maybe the reason you're not with your soulmate is because of your unwillingness to take a risk?

Or perhaps whenever you are in a relationship you are constantly worried about losing someone you love. If you continually fear losing a relationship, you have already lost it—if your belief is so great, you can actually make it happen.

Let go of the fear. Nothing inhibits love more than fear. The past doesn't have to control your future. Giving up the past is the key to inner freedom. Heal and let go of the old with love as you move into the new.

Learn to love again and open your heart fully in compassion, forgiveness, and unconditional love. If you can do this you will be a step closer to meeting your meant-to-be love.

Spiritual Health

In this fast-paced, highly stressed world it is very important to incorporate regular relaxation and spiritual practices into our lives. To achieve optimum health we must achieve harmony of mind, body, and spirit by making changes to the whole person.

Spend a few minutes of your day in solitude. Quiet your mind, become calm, and listen to the small voice within you. You can take an aromatherapy bath, read an inspirational book, escape to a quite place, go for a nature walk, or light a few aromatherapy candles and play some relaxing music. You can meditate or pray, practice yoga, or just relax. This is a time to recharge your spirit and clear your mind of all worries.

Whatever you decide to do, do it for at least 20 minutes on most days of the week, and you will start to notice that you feel less confused and scattered and you are more focused. When you are more focused, your ability to make correct decisions is greatly enhanced.

Look Good to Feel Good

Sadly, many young men and women don't think they are good-looking enough to attract their ideal mate. This is simply not true. It is not only people with movie star looks who are blessed with soulmate relationships. Just look around you—I bet you will see many normal people with loving relationships. Your ideal mate does not expect perfection.

If, however, you are not happy with some aspects of your appearance, now is the time to change them. People who care enough to take good care of themselves portray an admirable sense of self-worth. They have that bounce in their step and that sparkle in their eyes that is hard to miss.

People who respect themselves respect their bodies. By always looking your best, you tell people how you feel about yourself. Self-reliant, confident people are happy being who they are. They accept what they cannot change and change what they can.

JOANNE B. PARROTTA

Making the Most of Your Looks

You can make the most of your looks by overcoming particular beauty problems and finding a look that really suits you. Remember to set realistic goals instead of trying to live up to the unrealistic images that bombard us everyday in magazines and on television. Your goal should be to be the best you can. You have to feel comfortable in your own skin.

You don't have to look like a super model for your meant-to-be love to be attracted to you. What is important, however, is that you always look neat, from your clothes to you hair and nails, even down to your shoes.

Ask yourself a few simple questions:

1. Do your clothes flatter your body? How you present yourself to the world says a lot about you, so pay attention to what you're saying.
2. Is your hairstyle outdated? You'd be amazed at how a good style, and maybe a new hair colour, can make you look and feel.
3. Is your hair damaged and dry? Beautiful, healthy hair can do wonders for your looks and your confidence. Keep your hair clean and well conditioned to avoid dryness or frizziness.
4. Is your body always clean? Although this goes without saying, you would be surprised at how many people don't get it. A daily shower or bath will help control body odour and perspiration. Although a little perfume or cologne is nice (be careful not to overdo it), nothing is as seductive as that natural, just-showered scent.
5. Does your breath smell fresh? Brushing morning and night and flossing regularly will help keep your teeth

healthy and your breath smelling sweet. Visit your dentist every six months for a professional cleaning and check-up.

Your Face

The face is the most immediate expression of a person's beauty. This is why, whether you are a man or a woman, soft, supple, blemish-free skin is one of your greatest beauty assets. Although your genes determine your actual skin type, there is plenty you can do to ensure it always looks as good as possible. While you can spend a great deal of money and time looking after it with creams, lotions, cleansers and special treatments, in order for it to function well and look beautiful, you must start from the inside out.

Skin is a living, breathing thing made up of cells, and cells need nutrients to thrive. Thus, great skin starts with a healthy lifestyle. Proper gentle cleansing, toning, and moisturizing twice a day, along with plenty of sleep, a nutritious diet, and plenty of pure water, are a must. You should also avoid smoking and limit your exposure to sun and stress.

Ladies, if you wear makeup, please keep it subtle. Use it to enhance your natural beauty, not to hide it. Heavy makeup just makes you look like you're trying too hard and that's not very attractive. If you need help with makeup application, visit a professional in your department store cosmetic department. She or he can help you customize a natural look that best suits you.

Whether you are a man or a woman, looking and feeling good empowers you and gives you confidence. This will make you more likely to catch your soulmate's eye.

JOANNE B. PARROTTA
Eat Well to Live Well

A good diet has tremendous effects on health and beauty. Your skin and your hair, your body and your brain are all made up of the foods you eat. There is no doubt that they affect your physical health, mental health, and well-being. Making wiser dietary choices will not only reduce your risk of diseases but also will help you feel more confident. When you look and feel good, you have an unmistakable inner glow to which your loving soulmate will be attracted.

Eating well means eating a wide variety of properly prepared, healthy foods that you enjoy. A healthy diet consists of whole grain foods, such as whole-wheat bread, pasta, and crackers, and brown rice; eggs; chicken; fish; vegetables (especially dark leafy ones, such as spinach and bok choy); fruit; legumes (beans); and a daily multivitamin. Eat starches in moderation, especially if you're trying to lose weight. Always keep healthy snacks around, like those listed below, to help stave off hunger and keep you from grabbing a candy bar, doughnut, or soda pop when hunger hits.

- low fat yogurt
- a piece of cheese and a few pieces of fruit or vegetables
- a small handful of nuts
- a small cup of a clear vegetable soup or broth.
- a small salad

Eliminate, or at least limit, alcohol, coffee, and soda pop. Replace margarine with olive oil and small amounts of butter, and limit red meat and simple and refined carbohydrates, such as white flour, white sugar and its products, and all junk foods.

If you are overweight, you can begin to shed pounds simply

by cutting out junk food and eating three small, nutritionally balanced meals a day, plus two or three healthy snacks between meals. Make sure you drink plenty of pure water and get ample fresh air and exercise.

Exercise is essential to your health, whether you want to lose weight or not, and it will help you to stay within a healthy weight range. It will also tone your muscles and improve your circulation, and make your bones, joints, and ligaments stronger so they have a natural resistance to injury. Whatever form of exercise you choose to do—running, jogging, brisk walking, dancing, swimming, or bicycling—do it for 30 to 60 minutes at least three days a week.

Cleanliness Is Next to Godliness

Now that we've learned how to take care of our bodies inside and out, there is one more important issue I'd like to mention before I end this chapter—taking care of our homes. We have all heard the saying, "Your home is a reflection of you." If this is true, what does your home say about you? Your personal environment is an expression of your emotional inner being; how you keep your home can greatly influence how people treat you.

According to the ancient Chinese discipline of Feng Shui (which means "wind and water") a cluttered, disorganized home can create problems and obstacles in all areas of your life, including your relationships. Clutter can block the beneficial *chi* (cosmic energy or aura) from spreading easily throughout the house and can affect you physically, mentally, emotionally, and spiritually.

We all collect too much stuff, most of which we don't

really use or need. Karen Kingston, author of *Clear Your Clutter with Feng Shui*, says, "A major clear-out is absolutely essential if you truly want to have passion, joy, and happiness in your life." Reduce mental stress by clearing all unnecessary belongings from your home and organizing the rest. Create a home that serves your needs and dismiss the belief that more is better. Some people find that clearing the clutter provides an immediate sense of release and an increase in vitality, freedom, creativity, and energy.

I'm not suggesting that your home should be spotless all the time, but it should be reasonably clean and free from dust, mould, dirt, and clutter. Have a good spring cleaning every six months and get rid of—or better yet, recycle—anything you haven't used in about a year. If you haven't used it in that long, the odds are you probably never will.

In my book *A Return to the Simple Life: The Busy Woman's Guide to Restoring Balance, Health, and Beauty*, I guide my readers through the process of uncluttering their homes and their lives. I describe in detail the benefits of spiritual health, weight control, and healthy eating and living, plus I give some quick, healthy recipes for the busy cook. I also share many beauty techniques and tips that I picked up during my many years as a licensed beauty consultant. Instructions on how to order this volume are at the back of this book. Check it out.

A soulmate is someone who has the locks to fit our keys, and the keys to fit our locks. When we feel safe enough to open the locks, our truest selves step out and we can be completely loved for who we are; we can be loved for who we are and not for who we are pretending to be.

Each of us unveils the best part of one another. No matter what else goes wrong around us, with that one person we're safe in our paradise. Our soulmate is someone who shares our deepest longings, our sense of direction.

When we're two balloons, and together our direction is up, chances are we've found the right person. Our soulmate is the one who makes life come to life.

— Richard Bach

CHAPTER 4
MANIFESTING YOUR SOULMATE

Become aware that there are no accidents in our intelligent universe. Realize that everything that shows up in your life has something to teach you.

— Dr. Wayne W. Dyer

Just wishing for your soulmate is not enough. Your wishes can become a reality only when you are clear on what you truly want and need in a relationship. It is extremely important to know yourself well, to think long and hard about what makes you happy, and to look for someone with qualities that will support your happiness. You must know what you want before you can have it.

Most people don't know what characteristics they want in a mate. Before going any further, think about what kind of person you would like to be with. Keep in mind that relationships are mirrors in which we see ourselves. In order to find those ideal qualities in your soulmate, you must first be able to see them in yourself, or you will not be able to connect.

In this part of the book I show you how you can manifest your special someone and assist you in making the dream a reality.

Making the Dream a Reality

Write a list of the characteristics you want in your mate,

and be very specific. Set high yet realistic expectations. People who know that they deserve the best usually get the best. By valuing our own wonderful qualities, we have a good chance of connecting with our chosen one.

In working on this list, you must also be practical. Focus on this person's characteristics, not on your ideal man or woman—there is a difference. For example, you will notice that in the stories below, Jane did not wish for a man who is six feet tall with dark hair, a slim build, and green eyes, and James did not wish for a woman who looks like a top model.

Remember that our soulmates are usually not the type of person to whom we are normally attracted. Of course, that does not mean that your soulmate is not going to be attractive, if that's important to you. But instead of being tall and dark with green eyes, he or she may be shorter and blonde with blue eyes.

One word of caution before you start your list: there is no doubt that good looks make a great first impression, but they alone should not be of primary importance. Remember that the man who is good looking today may not be so great looking when he loses his hair and gains 30 pounds. Physical attraction can be short lived, but inner beauty will last a lifetime.

First, make a list of characteristics that you would like your soulmate to have. Here are some examples:

- Educated
- Ambitious
- Good looking
- 28–35 years old
- Catholic
- Spiritual
- Humorous

- Generous
- Intelligent
- High morals
- Loyal
- Honest
- Affectionate
- Passionate
- Loves animals and children
- Positive attitude
- Faithful
- Never been married
- Financially secure
- Successful
- Kind, gentle, and respectful
- Likes to travel
- Adventurous
- Family oriented
- Non-smoker

Next, circle or highlight the characteristics on which you will *not* compromise. For example, it may be very important to you that you soulmate have high morals and a sense of humour and be family oriented and spiritual. Finally, put it all together in a short paragraph.

Check out the wish lists written by Jane and James.

Jane's Wish List

I want a good looking, classy, intelligent man, who is between the ages of 28 and 35; someone who is sensitive and emotional, yet strong and masculine enough to take care of his own life. I would like him to be family oriented and love children, a man with high morals whom I can love and respect and who feels the same way about me.

JOANNE B. PARROTTA

I want someone who treats me like an equal and does not take me for granted. I want a man that likes adventure and travel, someone who is fun to be with and loves having a good time. He does not necessarily have to be religious, but I would like him to be in touch with his spiritual side, someone who lets my spirit and his run free. I want a soulmate who will be not only my lover but also my best friend.

James' Wish List

I want a soulmate who is between the ages of 25 and 30 and is ready to settle down and start a family. I want someone who is loving, generous, and kind, who loves family and children. I desire a classy woman who is strong, self-sufficient, can take care of herself, and is not needy in any way. I would like someone I can be proud to call my wife.

Now it is your turn. What is your wish list? Write it down. I have provided two blank pages for your convenience.

A MATTER OF DESTINY

THE CHARACTERISTICS I WOULD LIKE MY SOULMATE TO HAVE:

_____
_____
_____
_____
_____
_____
_____
_____
_____
_____
_____
_____
_____
_____
_____
_____
_____
_____
_____
_____
_____
_____
_____
_____
_____
_____
_____
_____
_____
_____

JOANNE B. PARROTTA

Read your paragraph every night before going to bed. Believe that this person exists and imagine what it would be like to be with him or her. Bring your five senses into play and fuel it all with passion.

Now that you are clear on the characteristics you want your soulmate to have, date different people. Stay positive and do not put your life on hold—live your life and work on bettering yourself. Obsessing over your soulmate will actually hinder your progress.

Eventually you will hit the mark; if you have done the necessary work it will likely to be within a year. Keep in mind that you are meant to be with your soulmate, but only when you both are ready. When the time is right, and usually when you least expect it, you will meet and you'll be amazed at how close he or she is to your wish list.

How Your Angels Can Help You Find Your Soulmate

Who, or what, are angels? They are spiritual beings, without earthly bodies, who serve as messengers of our Creator.

Do you believe in angels? Brad Steiger, author of *Guardian Angels and Spirit Guides*, reports that, according to a study conducted by *Time* magazine in 1993, 69 percent of Americans believe in the existence of angels, and 32 percent claim that they have personally felt the presence and guidance of these loving heavenly helpers.

Angels, true unsung heroes, are the embodiment of selfless devotion, limitless patience, and unconditional love. While they live in the spirit world, they spend a lot of time on earth, helping the person they were assigned to guide. Their job is to protect us and to help us fulfill our destiny in our spiritual, personal, and professional lives. They provide insight, awareness, support, and encouragement. However, they cannot interfere with our life lessons and our free will.

We all have more than one guardian angel; each one helps us in a specific area of our lives. The angel who guides your personal life will be the one who will help you and your meant-to-be love come together. How do they do this? By orchestrating the circumstances that bring soulmates together. Our wonderful heavenly helpers can intervene on our behalf in a number of ways such as telepathy, clairvoyance, intuition, vivid dreams, visions, and on rare occasion, even out-of-body experiences.

Ask and look for acknowledgement and signals, and when they come, don't discount them. Signals come in many forms—symbols, written signs, dreams, a paragraph in a book, a message in a song. Be aware of symbols that have meaning for you.

Your angels are likely to communicate with you in a much more subtle way such as knowingness, which is delivered through your thought processes. Knowingness is that subtle little voice inside our heads that most of us ignore. Or your angel may communicate with you through imagery in your dreams. Learning to interpret your dreams will provide you with a wealth of information.

Look beyond what is physically in front of you and call on the angels or a higher power to assist you in your search for love. These entities create miracles in the lives of a lot of people every day; allow them to create miracles in your life. All you have to do is acknowledge them and invite them to share your life, talk to them, and ask them to help you in your search for your soulmate. Remember, your life angels have been building a relationship with you since you were a baby and they will continue to do so for the rest of your life.

You will notice that when you let your angels into your life, you'll become sensitive to their presence. Their guidance will become more evident, revealing more information to you. As your relationship with your angels improves, you will also start to raise your personal vibration to a higher level and will find that the occurrence of synchronicities in your life increases. Enjoy your angels; they are a blessing and a delight.

Your Destiny and Your Connection with Your Soulmate

Meeting your loving soulmate really is *a matter of destiny*. Therefore, you should not worry about where and when you will meet this special person. Your spiritual guides (angels) are always working on bringing you together and will take care of the details. If it's in your destiny to be with your soulmate in this lifetime, you will meet, and until you do, you will continue to crave that soulful connection and will not feel completely fulfilled in other romantic relationships.

How do you know if it is in your destiny to meet your soulmate? If you have a strong desire to find and be with your mate and if your soul truly longs for that special connection, then chances are very high that it's in your destiny.

Nowadays many people are on a spiritual path, and are seeking more from life and from their relationships. They crave loving partnerships that go beyond the normal relationship. In this new age they will no longer tolerate disharmony in their relationships; their souls now yearn for that special someone to whom they feel deeply and spiritually connected.

What is unfortunate, however, is that most of us miss out on this special connection, usually because we are in such a hurry to be in love that we marry at a young age and settle for second best (karmic soulmates). While some people who are confident and emotionally mature meet their soulmates at a young age, most of us do not.

I have found that people who marry later in life have a better chance of meeting their loving soulmates than those that marry at a very young age. And these marriages seem to be more satisfying. Therefore, I advise young people to postpone marriage until they learn more about what love and relationships are all about and until they are sure they're with your destined love. Real love cannot be rushed. You must have maturity and wisdom before you can connect with your beloved.

If you're not with your loving soulmate at this time, don't despair; the timing is just not right yet. Maybe you still have a few more lessons to learn, so that when you do meet you'll appreciate the relationship, or maybe you are both in other relationships at this time. If you are sure that you're not with your soulmate and you are not happy and fulfilled in your present relationship, it is best to free yourself so that your destined love can come into your life.

I know that many of you who already have wonderful qualities—who are kind, loving, caring, and giving—have still not found the love of your life. Please don't get down on yourself. I ask you to be patient—perhaps there are more experiences you need to go through first. Once you meet your loved one you will understand why the delay was necessary. Compromising your dreams, goals, values, and lifestyle just to be with someone will only make you very unhappy. Settling is never the answer.

A MATTER OF DESTINY

Know in your heart that your spiritual partner is out there. Don't get discouraged if you haven't found him or her yet. Instead, get excited! This just means you have something wonderful to look forward to.

If love was a choice, who would ever choose to feel such exquisite pain?

— *Anna and the King*

CHAPTER 5
MEETING YOUR WONDERFUL SOULMATE

You think you might have met your soulmate, but how can you be sure? How do you differentiate between that special someone and other kinds of soulmate relationships? What are the characteristics that you're looking for in order to find true love? This chapter will answer these questions and many others.

How to Recognize Your Loving Soulmate

Your loving soulmate is very different from anyone else with whom you have had a relationship. He or she inspires a different kind of feeling and will radiate a different kind of energy. When you meet there will be an instant bond, resulting in an immediate trusting kindness. You will feel familiar, comfortable, at ease, completely happy, and fulfilled when you are together.

You might expect to feel intoxicated when meeting your soulmate, but this is more characteristic of karmic love relationships than of true soulmate ones. Most people feel a deep connection and an immediate affection for their soulmate. While for some meeting a soulmate may be love at first sight, for everyone it is "like at first sight." You will share a very special bond and your loving kindred spirit will make an impact on you.

A loving soulmate relationship may start out as a friendship. However, the attraction will grow stronger and more passionate as you get to know one another.

Your loving soulmate will support all of your deepest hopes and dreams, and will never try to change you in any way. His or her love is truly ever-present and completely unconditional. He or she will share your burdens, disappointments, and joys. True soulmates always place a high priority on each other's feelings.

If you suspect that you have found "the one," ask yourself these questions to be sure:

- Does this person love you unconditionally?
- Does he or she make you feel loved, respected, and special?
- Do you feel comfortable and at ease with him or her?
- Do you communicate at a deep soul level?
- Can you talk to each other about anything?
- Do you feel complete and content with this person most of the time?
- Do you share a common destiny (want the same things out of life)?
- Are you more powerful as a team than you were apart?
- Has the quality of your life improved since you met?
- Do you feel content and fulfilled in life?

If you answered *yes* to most of these questions and if your partner has the important characteristics on your wish list, then congratulations! You're with your loving soulmate.

But if you answered *no* to most of these questions, then you are not with your soulmate. You are not with your true love if the following statements are true:

- He or she does not support your hopes and dreams.
- He or she is a major cause of stress in your life.
- He or she does not fit in nicely in your life.
- He or she is not caring and considerate of your feelings and the feelings of others most of the time.
- He or she has more bad qualities then good ones.
- You have lost your identity and given up on your dreams.
- You have serious doubts about your relationship.
- There's too much drama in your relationship.

A word of caution: Be aware that we will not see unless we are ready to. Sometimes only one soulmate feels the connection, and the other may take a while. Patience is called for.

When and Where Can We Find Our Soulmates?

Louise L. Hay, a metaphysical teacher, lecturer, and bestselling author, says, "Love comes when we least expect it, when we are not looking for it. Hunting for love never brings the right partner. It only creates longing and unhappiness."

This of course doesn't mean you should sit at home and wait. It's very unlikely that your true love will come knocking on your door, unless your soulmate is your postage carrier or delivery person. You must be active and live life to the fullest. You do not need to do anything special to attract this special person—you just need to show up. He or she may be just around the corner, but if you don't get out of your house and actually turn that corner, you cannot connect.

Soulmates almost always meet in strange ways or while doing things that are out of character or visiting places that they wouldn't normally visit. So you must get out there and live a full life. It is time to stop waiting for love and start actively moving towards it. Get involved in your community, take courses, pursue a new hobby, join a fitness club, attend parties, try new activities, and be happy, active, and sociable.

You and your beloved will come together at the right time, in the right place and space for both of you. So, don't fuss; live your life, because when you are busy living your life, your beloved will magically appear.

Patrick's Story
In the last couple of years I have dated some wonderful women. They were all beautiful, smart and a lot of fun to be with and I was very attracted to them, but something just did not feel right. There was something missing with each one of them. I really didn't know what I was looking for, but I knew that I would know when found it.

Just when I had resigned myself to the fact that I would probably be single for the rest of my life, I was introduced to Pamela at a New Year's Eve party. We shook hands and exchanged a few words and then each went and mingled with the other guests. But for some reason I couldn't stop looking at her; she had the most amazing eyes I had ever seen. To my disappointment, she left the party early. As she was leaving our eyes met one last time and she flashed me the sweetest smile I had ever seen. The rest of the evening was a complete blur to me. All I could do was think about this mysterious lady, even though she was not the type of woman I would normally be attracted to.

Over the next few months I often found myself thinking about that beautiful brunette with those mesmerizing eyes. Then one spring evening I decided to stop and grab a bite to eat at a restaurant on my way home from work. Lo and behold, that mysterious woman from the New Year's Eve party was sitting in the booth right next to me, reading a newspaper while waiting for her meal. I quickly walked over to say hello. This time I was not going to let her get away.

I got up the nerve to ask Pamela to join me for dinner and she agreed. We spent the rest of the evening talking about anything and everything. She was so easy to talk to, and it was as if I had known her all my life. By the end of the evening we both knew we had finally found our life partner. Pamela and I married one year later.

If there is a lesson to be learned from Patrick's story, it is that we shouldn't settle for second best. We can't rush love. Patrick could have easily settled for one of the many women he was dating. But deep inside his soul, he knew there was something missing. He met Pamela when he had resigned himself to the fact that he might never find what he was looking for, and the soul connection was immediate.

Patrick mentioned that he was attracted to Pamela's eyes. This is a common characteristic of soulmate relationships—perhaps not too surprising, since they do say that the eyes are the windows to the soul.

Let's review what we've learned so far about *how*, *when*, and *where* you can meet your soulmate:

How Do I Meet My Soulmate?

The first step to meeting your soulmate is to learn to love and respect yourself. If you lack real self-esteem, are constantly putting yourself down, and aren't happy with who you are and the direction your life is taking, then you have some work to do. Only when you are secure in yourself can you hope to connect with your proper soulmate.

JOANNE B. PARROTTA

Tony's Story

I knew from the moment I first laid eyes on Marisa that I had just met my soulmate and the woman I was going to marry. People ask me how I knew, but it's hard to explain. When I was with her I felt comfortable and at peace, as if I had known her all my life. Although I was confident with myself and happy with my life before I met Marisa, there always seemed to be something missing. Now I know that Marisa was the missing piece to the puzzle.

Tony's description of how he felt when he met Marisa is a very common one. He just knew that she was the one—it really is that simple. Notice also that he connected with his kindred spirit when he was in a good place in his life. She was the only missing piece.

When Will I Meet My Soulmate?

You will meet your soulmate when you are both properly prepared and ready for the relationship. You first need to work on your own personal growth so that this intense love connection can take place. We can say that your ideal mate will come into your life when you need him or her the least.

This special person cannot enter your life if you are needy and greedy or feeling negative about your life and yourself. Ask yourself, "Am I ready to give and receive love generously and unselfishly, and am I the kind of person my true love can really love and respect?" If not, then you have some work to do. Real love comes only when you recognize your worth and you trust, respect, admire, and care for yourself and others.

As you better yourself, you begin to raise your personal vibration to a higher level. Your soulmate will be attracted to your new vibration. This kind of inner glow will light a fire inside of you that will be impossible for our beloved to resist.

A MATTER OF DESTINY

Where Will I Meet My Soulmate?

You can meet your soulmate almost anywhere. It might be at a social function, at work, through a mutual friend, or even in cyberspace. To increase your opportunities, you must stay positive, keep active, and live your life to the fullest. Go places, contemplate the beauty of nature, accept invitations, get involved in your community, take a course, make an effort to talk to new people, and let new people approach you (don't be timid, now). Keep in mind that every event you attend or person you meet can bring you one step closer to meeting your true love. Most importantly, smile, smile, smile! It makes you much more attractive, and you will eventually be noticed by that special someone.

Marriage is miserable unless you find the right person that is your soulmate and that takes a lot of looking.
— Marvin Gaye

CHAPTER 6
DATING IN ORDER TO FIND YOUR SOULMATE

Dating with Confidence

What does dating really mean? Dating simply means getting to know someone and letting him or her get to know you. Okay, it can be a little scary and maybe even a little complicated if you are not prepared for it. It can be uncomfortable if you don't know what to expect. However, successful dating can be wonderfully exciting, romantic, and fun, and it is a great way to meet different people—possibly even your soulmate. Don't take dating too seriously. Remember, it should be fun!

While you should enjoy getting to know new people, be selective. You don't have to date everyone who asks you out—there should be some chemistry there. Remember that you are dating in order to find your soulmate and to settle into a committed relationship or marriage.

You should have a pretty good idea within the first two dates as to whether this person is worth pursuing. If you have doubts about whether this person is the one for you, than he or she probably is not. He or she may be fun, smart, and a wonderful person. He or she may make a great partner for someone, but just not for you. If you're not feeling it, you're not feeling it—so don't force it. Move on, unless of course, you both want to remain friends.

If you know right from the start what your dating expectations are, you avoid wasting a lot of precious time. Don't compromise; decide what you need and want from a relationship and date different people until your needs are met. Remember that your soulmate is someone who will add to your life, rather than detracting from it.

Always believe that your soulmate can show up at any time, but don't put your life on hold. Your single years should be some of the most memorable and enjoyable years of your life. And remember that when you date with the intent of finding your soulmate, you send a message out into the universe that will act like a magnet, and the universe will bring your soulmate to you.

Internet Dating

Many people ask me whether they can meet their soulmates on the Internet. Of course the answer is yes. Internet matchmaking services can provide opportunities for meeting people that were unavailable in the past, but please proceed with caution.

The same principles that apply to in-person dating apply to Internet dating: be extremely careful about exchanging personal information such as your phone number and where you live until you feel you can totally trust this person. If you decide to meet, do so in a public place and always tell someone where you are going and when you expect to be back.

Know what you're looking for and never compromise. And while you can meet many people on the Internet, I don't suggest sitting at your computer for hours on a Saturday night chatting to strangers when you could be out at a social function having a good time and meeting people.

Only Fools Rush In

Why are most of us in such a hurry to get emotionally involved in a relationship? We jump in too quickly and come to the conclusion that we are in love much too soon.

A lot of singles, upon meeting someone they like who shows an interest in them, start a relationship right away instead of dating different people. They convince themselves that this is "the one" without giving serious thought as to whether this person is right for them. Some people take more care in choosing a new car than they do in choosing a mate.

Slow down! Don't allow yourself to get so swept away that you lose sight of you goals and your values. Know in your heart that your soulmate is looking for you. If you keep getting into and out of relationships that are not suitable for you, you are delaying the process of meeting your spiritual partner.

When you first start seeing a new person, be on guard and pay very close attention to your gut feelings and to any warning signs. It is your responsibility to make the right choices. Don't let loneliness or lust cloud your good judgment and don't mistake physical attraction for true love.

When you meet someone you like, I advise you to really get to know each other and become friends first before committing to a serious relationship; this may take more than a few months. Consider the fact that we are all on our best behaviour at the beginning of a relationship. Wait until the honeymoon phase is over before you become too emotionally or sexually involved. Do it right this time—by rushing, you lose the ability to be objective. You may end up in the wrong relationship, which will only delay your meeting with your true love.

What to Look For

A healthy relationship is based on the fact that we share ethical and spiritual values and a common destiny. Although soulmates often have different interests, they share similar values. Different interests can make for an interesting relationship, but different belief systems can make life very difficult. Extreme differences can cause major problems in your relationship and are a sure sign that you're not with your soulmate.

Characteristics to Avoid

In Chapter 2, I discussed the characteristics of bad relationships. In many cases, warning signs—some obvious and some not—of what is to come are evident during the start-up phase of the relationship, but we get so caught up by the excitement that we completely blind themselves to the other person's flaws. We try to justify, explain, or ignore the signs.

During the start-up phase of a relationship, you should gather as much information as possible about the person you're dating and pay close attention to any warning signs. Remember that the ability to foresee consequences before you act is a mark of a perceptive person.

The following are some warning signs to watch out for. If you are already involved with a person with one or more of these characteristics, you should seriously consider getting out of the relationship, especially if your partner doesn't agree to get help (see Chapter 2).

Warning Signs

Destructive habits: Avoid dating anyone who is hooked on drugs, alcohol, sex, or gambling. Even if they get help they are susceptible to developing new addictions. Remember that these individuals are very good at concealing their addiction. Be on the alert!

Bad temper: Moody people can be loving and kind one minute and angrily turn on you the next if things don't go their way. They may be very immature. While they can be very apologetic after one of their episodes, they may eventually abuse you in some way. Don't accept this behaviour, and don't believe them when they say they will never do it again. They most certainly will.

Extreme jealousy: Reasonable jealousy is a natural emotion which we all experience from time to time and should not cause major problems in a relationship as long as it is kept under control. However, being involved with an intensely jealous person can make your life a living hell. If your partner checks up on you, distrusts you, frequently shows up unexpectedly at your home or work, or insists on spending all of his or her free time with you and gets upset if you do anything that does not involve him or her, then you should be suspicious. Don't mistake jealousy for love. A person who does not trust you is usually someone who can't be trusted, and the situation will get much, much worse—perhaps even abusive—after you're married.

The need to be in control: Some people love to be in control of everything because they feel powerless and weak unless they are controlling someone else. This is a major red flag. Get out while you still can.

Domineering people need to be the boss. They tell you what to do and they expect to be obeyed. They may want to know where you are and who you're with at all times, even insisting that you carry a cell phone so that they can check up on you. They may get angry or abusive and threaten or bully you

If you're involved with a possessive and controlling person, you will eventually end up feeling unhappy and trapped in this relationship. Be aware that most of these individuals are very smart (in a conniving kind of way). They may control you in such a nice way that it won't seem like control. Don't be fooled.

Clinginess: Needy people will want to spend all their free time with you. They will come up with any excuse—even making them up—to justify being with you. When you can't be with them, they may still try to feel connected to you by asking you to do something for them.

Don't be flattered by the attention. Experts believe these individuals struggle with abandonment issues from childhood and probably didn't get enough attention or love from their families. Needy people may have adult bodies, but they are really children suffering from separation anxiety. They are usually loners who lack social skills and do not have a lot of friends. They may be uncomfortable in social situations and may come across as being insensitive and cold. They lack the necessary skills to maintain a healthy relationship and will not want to share you with anyone. You will eventually feel smothered and isolated in this relationship.

Cheating: We all have the right to insist on exclusivity in a relationship. Infidelity is a hard thing to forgive—not just the sexual act, but the betrayal and deceit, not to mention the risk of sexually transmitted diseases. It should not be tolerated. You will most likely never feel safe and secure in a relationship with someone who cheats.

Lying: Lying can be hard to detect. Good liars will tell you exactly what you want to hear and are very convincing. These people are very self-centred and often blame others for their problems. A person with very low self-esteem may lie to impress you. Lying can be contagious—if you spend enough time with a liar you may become a liar yourself.

Financial instability: Financial instability may indicate an addiction to shopping or gambling or just plain irresponsibility with money. These people are good at making excuses as to why they don't have any money. They constantly shift the blame onto others or some outside force. Sooner or later, they will ask to borrow money from you or even from your friends and family. Unless they get professional help, they will never be financially secure.

Cheapness: Some people are so cheap that they will avoid any situation in which they might be expected to pay. They always seem to "forget their wallet at home." While you should not expect your date to pay for everything all the time, there needs to be a balance. Before making any commitment, make sure that your potential partner's money style is compatible to yours.

Showing off: Love is never for sale. Don't be influenced by how much money someone has, never give in to material seduction, and do not accept expensive gifts at the beginning of a relationship. They are not appropriate and may make you feel obligated. Be aware that big spenders sometimes use money too impress others and to feel important. Barbara DeAngelis, Ph.D., best-selling author of *Are You the One for Me?* (a book I highly recommend), says, "When you choose a partner based on what he can offer you materially rather then what he can offer you emotionally, you will end up in the wrong relationship."

JOANNE B. PARROTTA

The Commitment Phobic

Many singles searching for lasting love have had their hearts broken once or twice by non-committers. While both men and women can be commitment phobic, it seems to be more prevalent in men.

Although they fear long-term relationships, non-committers often love the thrill of the chase. They will hold nothing back in trying to charm you and win your heart. They lavish you with gifts, compliment your every move, and smother you with attention. They are talented at making you feel extremely special. It is once they have won you over that the trouble begins.

There are various reasons why non-committers can't commit:

- **The thrill of the chase.** Some people are addicted to the excitement of a new relationship. Once they have won your heart they become restless and look elsewhere to get their next fix.
- **Fear of boredom.** Some people cannot commit to a lifetime with one person because they fear that their lives will become stale and boring. A committed relationship with this type of person is usually hopeless.
- **Always on the lookout for someone better.** A person like this spells trouble! He or she will have a hard time staying faithful and will dump you like a hot potato the minute someone else catches his or her eye. You deserve better.
- **Previous unsuccessful relationships.** Some people can't commit because they have been badly hurt in the past and fear having their hearts broken again.

With some patience and understanding, these individuals can eventually commit again. Try to help them to realize that you are different from their ex and that they can trust you. But don't waste a lot of time waiting for this to happen—get on with life.

Because they fear commitment, non-committers eventually destroy any solid relationship. Just when you think that the relationship is moving forward, they quickly shift into reverse. And it can happen so quickly and unexpectedly that you won't even see it coming.

Cindy's Story

I met Paul at a house party. It was an instant attraction for both of us. We talked and laughed for hours.

When we were dating, Paul said and did all the right things. You know, complements, roses, wonderful romantic dates, and love letters. He phoned me two or three times a day just to tell me he missed me and to say things like, "You're so beautiful and I am so lucky to have found you." It was incredible.

Paul would talk about the future using the word we, *making me believe that a future together was very possible. It seemed like we were meant for each other and I was so happy to have finally met my soulmate, or so I thought.*

Well, one Friday evening, about two months into our relationship, Paul called while I was getting ready to go on one of our amazing dates. I immediately sensed that something was wrong. Paul ended our relationship that night. His excuse: "This relationship is not working for me. I can't do this anymore. I am not ready for a long-term relationship right now, but please know that you are everything I ever wanted in a girl and I truly care about you. I am sorry if I hurt you, but we can be friends if you like."

It was all so unexpected. I just could not comprehend what had just happened. How could I have been so wrong? I really thought he cared about me and wanted a future with me. How could he say all those things and not mean them? How could I have been so stupid to fall for it?

Like Cindy, victims of non-committers are often left devastated by a great sense of loss. It is important for Cindy to realize that there was absolutely nothing she could have done differently to make the relationship work. If she is to heal from this she must release the anger and self-blame and move on.

Being involved with someone who can never fully commit to you can strike a blow to your self-esteem, which can take a long time to heal. Please don't fool yourself into thinking that you can change this person. Consider your loss another learning experience and move on. Know that true soulmates are always equally committed to the relationship and don't play games with people's feelings.

When searching for true love, remember that someone who seems too good to be true is just that: too good to be true. Look for a partner who possesses a good character, rather than just a good personality, who has integrity and shows you the respect you deserve. Don't waste your time and energy on someone who does not deserve your love.

Dating Do's and Don'ts

First impressions last a long time. By following some of these dating tips, you will greatly increase your chances of making a favourable first impression on your date.

- Always be friendly and lighthearted because you never know when your meant-to-be love will show up. Be responsive to another person's interest in you. If you appear to be too shy, cool, or aloof, you will seem unapproachable. And don't be afraid to show your interest. Relax, have fun, talk to people, and smile. When you flash someone a smile, you're sending him or her a signal that you are safe to approach.

- While you should be friendly, don't throw yourself at anyone. That only makes you seem desperate.
- Dress appropriately. We all judge people by the way they present themselves and your clothes say a lot about you. Don't send the wrong signal.
- If you are a smoker, consider quitting. Not only will it greatly improve your health, it will also improve your love life. Many singles are not be interested in dating a smoker.
- Be on time. It is extremely rude to keep people waiting.
- Don't use foul language, and pay close attention to how your date speaks. Using foul or inappropriate language on a regular basis is rude.
- On the first few dates, focus on fun and getting to know each other. Stay happy and positive and keep it light. Don't speak of marriage, children, or your future together, and don't bring up personal problems.
- There is no need to reveal everything about yourself on the first few dates—leave a little to the imagination. This makes you seem more mysterious and therefore more intriguing.
- Don't talk about sex on the first few dates. And refuse to answer personal questions that make you uncomfortable. If your date brings up the topic of sex

in your conversations, be on the alert. Sex may be all he or she wants.

- Be yourself when you're on a date. Relax and don't try too hard to impress. This is the only way you and your date can truly get to know each other.
- Everyone likes to be listened to. Be attentive, maintain eye contact, and listen to your date.
- Ask the right questions in order to access as much information as possible so that you can make intelligent decisions.
- Ladies, allow your date to wine and dine you without feeling guilty. A good man really does want to please a woman. Don't feel obligated to reciprocate; a sincere thank you will do. There will be plenty of time for you to do nice things for him if the relationship develops into a serious one.
- Men, as you probably already know, women love complements. But don't overdo it, and make sure the complements are sincere.
- Ladies, let the men do the courting and the pursuing. I know this sounds old school, but when it comes to love and sex, most men are old fashioned and are turned off when women come on too strong. Just because we are equal does not mean we are the same. Men like a challenge and like to pursue what they can't easily get. Don't play the game of hard to get, but don't be too aggressive.
- Resist the urge to engage in heavy make-out sessions on your first few dates. A warm hug or a light kiss is just fine. And, of course, no sex until you are madly in love and in a committed monogamous relationship.
- If your date does not call you or return your calls,

he or she is probably not interested in a relationship with you at this time. So don't wait by the phone. Get on with your life and date other people.
- Don't lead people on. If you are not interested in dating someone any longer, be honest. Thank your date for a wonderful evening and say that you don't feel that you're compatible enough or a good match. Being direct frees you both to continue looking for the right person.

The five biggest dating mistakes are (a) not asking enough questions, (b) making premature compromises, (c) having sex before commitment, (d) putting a commitment before compatibility, and (e) ignoring the warning signs of potential problems. Value yourself and your goal of finding a soulmate.

Dating Safety Tips for Women

Women need to be especially careful when dating. Here are some safety tips:

- Don't take risks with your safety. Always tell someone you trust where you are going, with whom, and when they can expect you back.
- Don't invite a stranger to your place, and don't go to his.
- Meet in a public place.
- Always have enough money with you in case he decides he is not paying for your dinner, and have an alternate transportation plan in case he refuses to take you home.
- Don't drink too much. Always stay in control so you can take care of yourself. And be aware that the date rape drug is still going strong.

- Pay attention and trust your instincts. If this person makes the hair on your body stand on end and your stomach is in knots, you should get the out of there. Tell him you're not feeling well and you need to go home. Don't except a ride; always be prepared to take a taxi.
- Some men expect sexual favours in exchange for dinner or a night on the town. Set these jerks straight right of the bat. You are not obligated in any way to grant sexual favours, for any reason.
- If things get violent and you must defend yourself, do so. Target the kneecaps, eyes, or crotch. Run and yell for help.

Sexual Responsibility

No relationship book would be complete without a few words on sexual responsibility. You may find that some of my views are a bit old fashioned—I can't help that. It isn't my intention to push my beliefs on anyone, so please take from this book only what feels good to you and discard the rest.

Sex and Commitment

Making love is a physical way to honour your love for each other. Sex with your true love can be a beautiful thing and is the only time when you can truly say that you are *making love* instead of just having sex. It requires trust, responsibility, and respect.

However, it is fairly common, even in this age of deadly sexually transmitted diseases (STDs), for singles to have sex during the early dating stage. Some justify it by saying that they are sexually liberated, yet they wonder why they have such a hard time finding and keeping someone who will commit to a serious relationship with them. Others may worry that if they don't have sex by the third or fourth date their date will lose interest in them and move on.

I truly believe that our liberal attitude towards love and sex has gotten us in a lot of trouble. STDs, divorce rates, abortion rates, and teenage pregnancies have increased tremendously. And although the threat of STDs like AIDS scares most people, casual sex is still thriving.

Our society is addicted to immediate gratification, and delaying sex is very difficult for a lot of people. But if we immediately indulge in our every desire, we miss out on the anticipation that builds. When we wait for the right time, the whole sexual experience will be more exciting and wonderful.

Having intercourse before you have achieved a spiritual and emotional connection will end up hurting you and your relationship. Becoming sexually involved too soon decreases the chances that the relationship will grow into a healthy and lasting one.

Safe Sex

When you feel the time is right to have sex, please take care of yourself and your partner by being sexually responsible. Have the safe sex talk. I know it won't be easy, but if you're embarrassed then maybe you don't know this person well enough to have sex with him or her. Insist that you or your partner uses birth control each and every time, but be aware that not all forms of birth control protect you from STDs such as AIDS, chlamydia, genital warts, herpes, syphilis, pelvic inflammatory disease, or gonorrhea.

Keep in mind just how dangerous STDs are. Some, like herpes, will stay with you forever; there is no cure. Others, like AIDS, are deadly. Chlamydia can cause infertility in women. Frightening statistics verify that people who have sex with multiple partners are at high risk of pelvic inflammatory disease, which can lead to lifelong infertility. In addition, research now shows that cervical cancer is most commonly caused by a sexually transmitted virus.

Put your health and safety before sex!

Love is friendship that has caught fire. It is quiet understanding, mutual confidence, sharing and forgiving. It is loyalty through good and bad times. It settles for less than perfection and makes allowances for human weaknesses. Love is content with the present, it hopes for the future, and it does not brood over the past. It's the day-in and day-out chronicle of irritations, problems, compromises, small disappointments, big victories and working toward common goals. If you have love in your life, it can make up for a great many things that are missing. If you don't have love in your life, no matter what else there is, it's not enough.

— Ann Landers

CHAPTER 7
SO YOU'VE MET YOUR SOULMATE

This final chapter will help you get ready for the journey that is ahead for you and your mate. You will learn various relationship skills and how to deal with some of the issues that inevitably come up in a committed relationship. But, before we get into all that, let's start by finding out what men and women really want from romantic relationships.

What Do Men Really Want?

Well, according to some of the professional men I interviewed when researching this book, most men like an independent women who has her own career, is health conscious and takes good care of herself, is not needy, and has her own interests and will allow them to have theirs. Paul, a 32-year-old accountant said, "I want a woman who loves me but doesn't always need me; someone who doesn't feel rejected when I want to spend time alone or with my buddies—someone who isn't too demanding of my time."

Don't take a man's need to spend time alone personally. A lot of the men I spoke to confessed that the more they are away from their loved ones, the more they miss and think about them. I guess there might be some truth to the old saying "Distance make the heart grow fonder." By allowing your man his space, you show him that you are an independent person who doesn't constantly need his attention, and that can only make you more attractive in his eyes.

It is very important that both partners in a relationship remain independent; this means spending a healthy amount of time apart, doing things with families and friends. Everybody needs their space and the quality of time we spend with our partner is more important than the quantity. I find that couples who spend too much time together often don't make an effort to spend time alone and they begin to take the relationship and each other for granted. Of course, neither of you should neglect the other or your relationship; your partner should always make you one of his first priorities.

A lot of women mistakenly think that men just don't want to be with an independent, professional woman because they feel threatened by their success. But that's exactly what your loving soulmate will be attracted to. Most good men (notice I said *good* men) do appreciate a woman who is independent and has her own career. Your mate will be proud of your achievements and encourage your career goals. Only an insecure man who doesn't have a lot of respect for women could be threatened by your successes.

Although most men find successful, strong, independent women very sexy and interesting, they like them to still look and act feminine. The men I interviewed made a point that they want a woman who takes good care of herself and keeps up her looks.

What I'm about to tell you next probably won't come as much of a surprise. The majority of the professional men I spoke to say that they want their strong and career-oriented woman to show some domesticity. Doing some of the things his mother may have done for him (cooking a nice meal and helping him keep the house clean and tidy) makes him feel loved and nurtured. After all, they feel that they are there for you when you need them to fix a leaky faucet or do some minor repairs on your car. Don't be afraid to do nice things for your partner as long as he is willing to do nice things for you and is appreciative of all you do.

Men's number-one complaint is about women who are controlling, complaining, criticizing, and whining. They cannot read your minds, so you must ask for what you want and need. All a good man wants is to be able to please you, but if you complain all the time, he will get discouraged and feel that nothing he does is ever good enough for you. Eventually he will stop trying to please. He will love you more if he feels he can make you happy, so try not to criticize or give unwanted advice.

Men appreciate positive attention and praise almost as much as women do. They love it when you complement them on their appearance or on whatever they do. So praise his good qualities instead of criticizing his faults. Tell him how glad you are that he is part of your life and how lucky you are to have him. Always let him know that you appreciate his efforts in trying to please you. Help him be successful in making you happy, and you will continue to reap the rewards.

What Do Women Really Want?

A woman, more than anything else, wants to be cherished by her man. She needs to feel that she is number one in his life and that he is madly in love with her, and she needs to be reassured of this on a daily basis. She needs him to be generous with his affections and to connect with her every day. It can be something as small as a loving look, a loving touch, or a gentle caress. Talk is cheap, and although a woman wants you to say

"I love you," what she wants and needs even more is for you to *show* her you love her.

Smart, independent women don't want macho men who talk down to them. They want men who genuinely like and respect them. When a guy likes women and is self-confident enough to treat a woman like a woman, it shows in his actions. He is attentive, respectful, and a gentleman. He knows that romance and communication are the keys to a good relationship and a great marriage.

Women want to be listened to and understood. It is also very important to honour their feelings. I know that emotions can sometimes make men feel a bit uncomfortable, but allow your partner to express herself and be there for her by offering her a shoulder to cry on when she needs one. Women also appreciate a guy who is not afraid to show his feelings, someone who is a little sensitive (without being wimpy).

Contrary to men, women need to talk things through. Walking away or refusing to deal with a situation or a conflict will further upset your partner and cause her to withdraw. Women need men who are willing to communicate their feelings and talk about any problems in the relationship. Unpleasant as it may be to you, respect her enough to listen to her opinion and deal with problems in a calm and gentle manner.

A woman needs her man to be manly, yet supportive, loving and encouraging. She wants a man who she can trust completely and who will make her feel appreciated, safe, and secure. She needs someone who cares about her well-being and supports her goals, on whom she can count in good times and in bad, and who is true to his word. Women want men to do nice things for them, but they don't want to have to tell them to do these nice things. Be spontaneous. An anniversary or birthday is not as special if she has to remind you about it. You must learn to read her signals and make an effort to remember special occasions.

It's unfortunate that a lot of men stop courting women after they are in a committed relationship. They have this absurd idea that they don't need to try hard any more. Big mistake! Their partners end up feeling used and taken for granted and eventually resent them. Show appreciation for all the things your wonderful lady does to make your life more comfortable. Treat her at all times like the lady you love and she'll treat you with the respect and love that you expect.

While there is no doubt that men and women are different in many ways, our basic human needs are the same. We all want to feel special and adored by our partners, to be accepted for who we are, and to be loved unconditionally, despite our imperfections.

To Have and to Hold

Congratulations! You have met someone whom you love, respect, and admire and about whom you are passionate. However, there is still no need to rush into a marriage. Take the time to make certain that you're with your right soulmate. You must get along well, want the same things out of life, and share a mutual respect and admiration for one another. You must love each other so passionately that you can't imagine your life without each other.

There must be no doubt in your mind that this is the person with whom you want to spend the rest of your life, nor should you have any unresolved issues. Problems will not automatically disappear after you're married; in fact, the opposite is usually true. Little problems become big ones and bad situations are always made worse. Just ask any married couple. Are you prepared to deal with that?

I am not trying to scare you, but it is very important to make a rational, intelligent decision when choosing a life partner. Happy marriages involve hard work and attention from both partners. It is a lifetime commitment, not a decision to be taken lightly. Ending a marriage involves tremendous pain and a tremendous sense of loss—not only for you and your partner, but also for your family and close friends.

If, after considering all these points, you believe that you've found your true soulmate, then you have a very good chance at a successful, happy marriage.

Before You Say "I Do"

The engagement period is a time to create lasting memories and to celebrate your love. This is also the time when you put everything out on the table and should come to agreements on any unresolved issues, such as how the finances will be handled, how you plan to raise and discipline your children, how the household chores will be shared and so on. These discussions will not necessarily be easy. Remember, love does not conquer all. But it is important to resolve these issues before you get married. You do not want any unpleasant surprises.

In this section I will address the three major issues that must be discussed:

1. money,
2. housework, and
3. children (with in-laws running a close fourth, but that's a whole other book).

A MATTER OF DESTINY

Money: What's Yours Is Mine

Money can be a touchy topic for couples. Money management is one of the toughest responsibilities of marriage and can be a source of conflict and a primary contributing factor to a marriage breakdown. However, problems can be avoided if you discuss your financial goals and style with your partner and come to an agreement before you tie the knot.

We can be very idealistic when it comes to money, denying its importance, especially when we're in love. Yet even soulmate relationships are not above money. Let's face it—we have to support ourselves and our children, now and in the future. Without money, we can't put our children through college, we can't prepare for our retirement, and we can't live those dreams of a better life—a life in which we are free of financial worries.

You must work as a team and be honest and responsible with your finances in order to achieve financial freedom. And if your objective is to accumulate sufficient savings so that you do not have to worry about money, you will need discipline, hard work, and courage, and you'll have to make some sacrifices along the way. Having a spending plan, living below your income, and saving and investing regularly is a sure way of creating abundance.

Housework as a Joint Venture

Surprising as it may sound, housework can become a serious issue in a marriage. An unwillingness to share in the housework shows a lack of respect for your spouse and will have a negative affect on your marriage over time. However, housework does not have to be divisive. Talk about how the household chores will be shared and be willing to be flexible.

I find that loving soulmate couples don't have as big an issue with shared domestic duties as do karmic soulmates. Loving soulmates are more evolved individuals who are in touch with both their male and feminine sides. They don't demean their partners by treating them like servants. They are fair and respectful and believe that if they both work outside the home, the housework should be equally shared.

Parenting Your Children

Before getting married, couples must discuss whether both partners want to have children and reach an agreement as to how they plan to parent their children. No two parents have the same parenting styles. If your styles don't complement each other and you are not consistent in enforcing the rules, your children will receive mixed messages and play one parent against the other. You must find a middle ground that works for everyone concerned. Your children will always benefit if you are able to achieve a well-balanced style that is firm, yet fair and a little flexible.

Parenting is a tough job, but fortunately it comes with great joys and many precious moments that make it all worthwhile. Develop realistic expectations about childrearing. Remember that there are no perfect parents and no perfect children; we simply do the best we can. Following are four tips that may help.

1. **Spend plenty of time with your children.** Parenting doesn't have to be a serious business all the time. What your children want most is your time and attention. Spend some time each day playing, teaching, talking, and having fun with your children.

2. **Love and care for them as best as you can.** Parental love gives children a sense of security, belonging, and support. Your love should be constant and unconditional. Children who are starved for love and affection will act out in a negative way.
3. **Discipline constructively.** As parents, it is our job not only to love our children but also to discipline them. We all want to raise children who will become loving, generous, responsible, moral adults. In order for your family to function properly, you must set and adhere to a standard of behaviour. Be consistent and never undermine the rules set by your spouse. Disagreements about rules should always be resolved in private, never in front of the children.
4. **Tend to your marriage needs.** Make your marriage your first priority. Happy parents are most apt to have happy well-adjusted children. The best gift we can give our children is the sense of security that comes from having parents who love and respect each other.

For Better or Worse

Life with your soulmate will not always be easy, and you're fooling yourself if you think that your partner will fulfill your every expectation. Your partner is human after all, and has his or her own issues to deal with. While the two of you will not always agree, get along, or act in loving way, marriage to your soulmate will not be difficult to maintain. In this type of relationship, divorce or separation is almost never an option.

The problems that do arise between loving soulmates are often caused by outside forces, such as money, family, or children, so try to stick together and agree to disagree! It's really not important to win every argument. Would you rather be happy or right? You decide.

It is, however, important that you maintain open lines of communication at all times with your loved one and discuss any problems as soon as possible. Don't wait until resentment builds or it could eventually destroy your marriage.

Learn to fight fair. Never accuse or blame your partner. Instead, gently express your hurt or angry feelings and tell them how their actions made you feel. Express your needs—don't expect your partner to read your mind. Be honest, but kind and sensitive to each other's needs and feelings. Sometimes we treat strangers with more courtesy than we do the people we love most.

The rare few loving soulmates who do decide to part do so in a positive, loving way and will always share a special bond. They will never stop loving each other, unlike those in karmic soulmate relationships, who might. Tell your partner that you will always be there for him or her no matter what and promise to never use demeaning, hurtful language no matter how bad things get.

You and your soulmate have lessons that you must learn together and you both require some relationship skills. But there will be no doubt whatsoever in your mind that you have found the love of your life. It will all just feel right and inevitable.

Laurie's Story

I know that a lot of people say that love at first sight is not a common occurrence among soulmates, but that's exactly what happened when Joe and I met at a baseball game through a friend of a friend. We both could not take our eyes off each other. Joe asked for my phone number and called me later that evening to ask me for a date the following Friday. I was overjoyed and could hardly wait for Friday to come along.

That was three years ago. Joe and I fell madly in love and married six months after we met. We both instinctively knew without a doubt that we had found our other half. Our romance was like a fairytale. We loved and respected each other so much and we never argued.

The first year of our marriage was wonderful. Joe had a great job at a major accounting firm and I was attending nursing school. But approximately two months after our first anniversary, Joe was unexpectedly laid off. Joe is a proud, hardworking man and took this loss very hard.

It took Joe six months to find another job, and in the meantime the bills piled up. We had no choice but to sell our small apartment, which we both loved. I had to put my studies on hold and find a job, which really upset Joe. He became increasingly depressed and withdrawn. His self-esteem plummeted. The fun and passion in our marriage was slowly deteriorating.

I could not believe what was happening to our fairytale marriage. We began to fight, which truly upset the both of us. Our money problems were tearing us apart. Money had never been a big issue in our lives before. Now that's all we could think about.

Things got so bad that I considered leaving, but I could not bring myself to do it. I still loved Joe with all my heart and soul and he still loved me the same way. For some reason our marriage and love were being tested, but in my heart I knew that if we just stuck with it, everything would work out.

Well, that's exactly what happened. Joe finally landed the job of his dreams and I am now in my last year of nursing school. We hope to have enough money put aside by next year to buy our own place and start a family. Our relationship has grown and become even stronger after our six months of hell. I believe it was our great love for each other that brought us through this very challenging time in our lives. We now know that we can overcome any obstacle.

As you can see from Laurie's story, even soulmates have serious issues to deal with. Just because you've found your true love does not mean that your life will always be wonderful. But Laurie and Joe never lost sight of the fact that they loved each other and that the problems they were experiencing were due not to their relationship, but to an outside force beyond their control.

It takes a great deal to upset a soulmate union. You may argue and fuss, but you will almost always overcome any obstacle that comes your way. While you have come together to learn lessons, keep in mind that your loving soulmate is not the lesson. Rather, you will help each other learn the lessons.

Don't Be Afraid to Apologize

I'm sorry. These two little words can be so powerful and meaningful. We all make mistakes; no one is perfect. To be willing to apologize is admirable because it means you take responsibility for your mistakes. With a heartfelt apology, just about anything can be forgiven.

Unfortunately, some people have such a hard time saying they were wrong that for them apologizing is like pulling teeth. Admitting your mistakes is not easy, but do it anyway. It gets easier over time and allows the healing process to begin. Apologizing when appropriate can create a stronger bond with your loved one and increase his or her trust in you.

Preparing for the Wedding

There is nothing more radiant than a truly happy bride and groom who have no doubts whatsoever that they are with their destined love. Their smiles and the look of love in their eyes is truly a wonderful sight.

Your wedding should be meaningful to both of you, so put thought and imagination into your plans. Involve the people who are important to you. Remember that a good wedding does not have to be lavish or expensive. What's most important is that it be fun and memorable.

While preparing for your perfect wedding can be exciting, it can also be stressful. Make sure you take good care of yourselves so that you will feel great and have lots of energy; eat well and find time to relax. And don't let your planning take over your relationship. Spend quality time together having fun and continuing to get to know each other.

Some Ways to Say "I Love You"

Everyone expresses love in different ways. While one person may show love by sending roses and a love note to work, someone else may express it by bringing coffee in bed in the mornings or making a nice dinner. Your partner may not communicate love the way you would like, but may still be very much in love with you. It is best to let go of fixed ideas about how your partner should articulate love.

There are hundreds of ways to say "I love you." The following list contains a few ideas to help trigger your imagination. As you'll see, being romantic doesn't have to cost a small fortune.

- Dedicate a song to your partner on his or her favourite radio station.
- Surprise your partner with a photo album or scrapbook of the two of you together.
- Leave a romantic message on his or her answering machine.

- Treat your loved one for a nice dinner and a scenic ride. For a special occasion like a birthday, anniversary, or Valentine's Day you could even rent a limo. Don't forget the champagne.
- Take a picnic dinner and a blanket to a park or the beach and watch the sunset.
- Hold hands while on a moonlit walk on the beach on a warm summer night.
- Enjoy a romantic candlelit dinner at home.
- Make hot chocolate and snuggle up near the fireplace.
- Send flowers to your partner at work with an affectionate note. It doesn't have to be a special occasion. It means so much more when it's "just because."
- Pamper your partner with a gift certificate to a health spa for a massage or facial.
- Write a poem, a love letter, or a song for your partner.
- Make sure you phone your partner when he or she is sick. Show concern.
- Make your special person king or queen for a day: clean the house, wash the car, serve breakfast in bed, etc.
- Plant a small tree or perennial flower in your yard every year on your anniversary and watch it grow and flourish, just like your love for each other.
- Leave little love notes all over the house.
- Create a romantic ambiance with a roomful of candles. Sip wine or champagne and snack on cheese and crackers, grapes, or strawberries.

A MATTER OF DESTINY

- Bake a heart-shaped cake and write "I love you" with icing.
- Buy or make a picture frame that says "Soulmates" for your favourite picture of the two of you.
- Surprise your partner with a sensual aromatherapy bath when he or she gets home late from work. See the instructions below.

A candlelit bath will create a sensual ambiance which will ignite passion, rejuvenate the body and the spirit, and float all your cares away.

1. Make sure the bathroom is warm.
2. Have two fluffy terry towels and robes ready.
3. Put on some relaxing music.
4. Pour yourself a drink, if you like.
5. Light at least 3 aromatherapy candles. You can make your own: using a paper towel, rub the outside of an ordinary candle with aromatherapy oils and add four or five drops to the melting wax of the candle. Be careful not to get oils on the flame or in your eyes.
6. Mix four drops of each of the following sensual aromatherapy oils in a tub of very warm water just before you're ready to get in: rose, lavender, and vanilla. (Rose petals and bath salts can also be added to the bath water but be careful not to plug the drain.)
7. Turn off the electric lights, ease yourselves into the warm water, and enjoy.

Make sure you're not interrupted for at least 30 minutes. Treasure this quality time with your loved one. Clear your minds of all worries, relax your bodies, close your eyes, and gently hold each other. Breathe deeply and take pleasure in this blissful experience. You deserve it!

Unconditional Love: The Key to a Successful Union

A relationship is a journey. It is always evolving and can at times be very difficult. Your love will be tested and you will have obstacles to overcome. The key to a successful, happy union is unconditional love. If you love each other unconditionally, you can overcome the struggle that you face together.

Nurture your love every day and life's inconveniences will be easier to cope with. Remember that unconditional love is kind, encouraging, mutually respectful, and compassionate. It is a love without conditions. By putting yourself in your partner's shoes, by showing compassion, patience, tolerance, and empathy, you can unlock the key to a healthy, loving relationship.

When you love each other in this way, your relationship will truly be made in heaven. Never forget that you are now a team. Live for each other and help each other along the way.

May your journey together be a magical one!

FILMS WITH SOULMATE THEMES

Somewhere in Time (1980)
Starring Christopher Reeve, Jane Seymour

Made in Heaven (1987)
Starring Timothy Hutton, Kelly McGillis

What Dreams May Come (1998)
Starring Robin Williams, Annabella Sciorra

Serendipity (2002)
Starring John Cusack, Kate Beckinsale

Just Like Heaven (2005)
Starring Reese Witherspoon, Mark Ruffalo

BIBLIOGRAPHY AND RECOMMENDED READING

Soul Mates and Twin Flames
by Elizabeth Claire Prophet
Summit University Press, 1999

Twin Souls: Finding Your True Spiritual Partner
by Patricia Joudry and Maurie D. Pressman, M.D.
Hazelden, 2000

The Bridge across Forever: A Lovestory
by Richard Bach
Dell, 1986

Soulmates: Following Inner Guidance to the Relationship of Your Dreams
by Carolyn Godschild Miller
H. J. Kramer, 2000

Soul Mates
by Richard Webster
Llewellyn Publications, 2001

Heart and Soul: A Spiritual Course for Meeting
by Rosemary Ellen Guiley, Ph.D.
Berkley, 2002

The Marriage Plan: How to Marry Your Soul Mate in a Year—or Less
by Aggie Jordan, Ph.D.
Broadway Books, 2000

Love is a Miracle: Amazing Real Life Stories of Matches Truly Made in Heaven
by Brad Steiger
Kensington, 2001

When God Writes Your Love Story: The Ultimate Approach to Guy/Girl Relationships
by Eric and Leslie Ludy
Multnomah, 2004

Guardian Angels and Spirit Guides: True Accounts of Benevolent Beings from the OtherSide
by Brad Steiger
Signet, 1998

How to Talk with Your Angels
by Kim O'Neill
Avon Books, 1995

Finding Your Soul-Mate
by Russ Michael
Weiser Books, 1992

Echoes of the Soul: The Soul's Journey beyond the Light—Through Life, Death, and Life after Death
by Echo Bodine
New World Library, 1999

A MATTER OF DESTINY

Soulmates: Honoring the Mysteries of Love and Relationship
by Thomas Moore
Harper Perennial, 1994

Soul Love: Awakening Your Heart Centers
by Sanaya Roman
H. J. Kramer, 1997

How to Uncover Your Past Lives
by Ted Andrews.
Llewellyn, 2002

What Happens after Death: Scientific and Personal Evidence for Survival
by Migene Gonzalez-Wippler
Llewellyn, 1951

The Power of Karma: How to Understand Your Past and Shape Your Future
by Mary T. Browne
HarperCollins, 2002

You Can Heal Your Life
by Louise L. Hay
Hay House, 1987

Bad Boys: Why We Love Them, How to Live with Them, and When to Leave Them
by Carole Lieberman and Lisa Collier Cool
Dutton, 1997

JOANNE B. PARROTTA

Clear Your Clutter with Feng Shui
by Karen Kingston
Broadway Books, 1999

Men Like Women Who Like Themselves (and Other Secrets That the Smartest Women Know)
by Steven Carter and Julia Sokol
Dell, 1997

Loving Him Without Losing You: How to Stop Disappearing and Start Being Yourself
by Beverly Engel
Wiley, 2001

Mars and Venus on a Date: A Guide for Navigating the 5 Stages of Dating to Create a Loving and Lasting Relationship
by John Gray, Ph.D.
HarperCollins, 1997

But I Love Him: Protecting Your Teen Daughter from Controlling, Abusive Dating Relationships
by Dr. Jill Murray
Regan Books, 2001

Are You The One For Me? Knowing Who's Right and Avoiding Who's Wrong
by Barbara DeAngelis, Ph.D.
Dell, 1992

Why Love Is Not Enough
by Sol Gordon, Ph.D.
Adams Media, 1990

Affirmations: Your Passport to Happiness
by Anne Marie Evers
Berkana Books, 1999

Fit for Love—Find Yourself and Your Perfect Mate
by Olga Sheean
Inside Out Media, 2005

What Men Want: Three Professional Single Men Reveal to Women What It Takes to Make a Man Yours
by Bradley Gerstman, Christopher Pizzo, and Rich Seldes
HarperCollins, 1998

The Trick to Money Is Having Some!
by Stuart Wilde
Hay House, 1995

ABOUT THE AUTHOR

Born in southern Italy, Joanne B. Parrotta now lives in Vancouver, BC. Since the beginning of the 1980s, she has been studying, learning, and writing about topics ranging from spirituality to personal growth. She writes books that will make a difference in people's lives.

Joanne's passionate interest in helping others began early in life. She has worked in a group home for troubled teens and volunteered at a support services organization for battered women, where she received several months of counselling training. She has happily provided a home for several foster children and has raised three of her own.

Now, through her writing, she reaches out to counsel others and share her wisdom and passions with her readers.

READERS' SUGGESTIONS

Joanne B. Parrotta is always gathering information that fits the spirit of *A Matter of Destiny* for possible inclusion in future editions. She invites her readers to share their own inspirational stories of destined love, including stories of karmic relationships, karmic marriages, Twin Soul relationships, and divine interventions (angels). She would love to hear from you.

Please e-mail your stories to stories@amatterofdestiny.com. Include your name, address, and e-mail. If your story is selected, you will be listed as a contributing author (or you may remain anonymous if you choose).

Thank you for sharing!

Note: Due to the overwhelming amount of e-mails I receive, it is unfortunately difficult to respond to every message. I do, however, read each and every one of them, so please keep in touch.

Check out Joanne's Web site at
www.amatterofdestiny.com

JOANNE B. PARROTTA

If you enjoyed **A Matter of Destiny**, *you may wish to read Joanne B. Parrotta's other book, coming soon.*

A Return to the Simple Life
The Busy Woman's Guide to Restoring Balance, Health, and Beauty

This book covers an extensive range of topics, from keeping life simple to good nutrition and weight control to almost everything you need to know about inner and outer beauty. *Return to the Simple Life* gives women solutions to the unavoidable challenges of modern life so they can improve the quality of their lives. It also teaches them how to take better control of their time and how to simplify their lives by reducing the number of steps necessary to complete everyday tasks.

For more information and to reserve this book, e-mail the author at info@amatterofdestiny.com or visit the author's website at www.amatterofdestiny.com

Give a Gift from the Heart!

We hope you have enjoyed reading *A Matter of Destiny*. Could someone you know benefit from reading it as well? It is the perfect gift for the single person looking for true love.

Visit the authors website at www.amatterofdestiny.com for instructions on how you can order more books.